D0816272

Vienna

Berlitz Publishing Company, Inc.

Princeton   Mexico City   London   Eschborn   Singapore

Text:	Jack Altman
Editor:	Media Content Marketing, Inc.
Photography:	Jack Altman pages 3, 4, 10, 11, 30, 38, 48, 65, 78, 86, 91, 93, 94, 96; Jon Davison pages 13, 19, 25, 26, 33, 36, 40, 43, 44, 47, 56, 61, 71, 74, 84; Jean-Claude Vieillefond pages 14, 20, 77, 88.
Cover Photo:	Jon Davison
Photo Editor:	Naomi Zinn
Layout:	Media Content Marketing, Inc.
Cartography:	Raffaele Degennaro

Although the publisher tries to insure the accuracy of all the information in this book, changes are inevitable and errors may result. The publisher cannot be responsible for any resulting loss, inconvenience, or injury. If you find an error in this guide, please let the editors know by writing to Berlitz Publishing Company, 400 Alexander Park, Princeton, NJ 08540-6306.

ISBN 2-8315-7709-8

Printed in Italy

030/107 RP

CONTENTS

- A (☛ in the text denotes a highly recommended sight

Vienna

VIENNA AND THE VIENNESE

Austria's venerable capital no longer sits on its laurels, but neither has it thrown them out. After years of bathing in the glow of an old worldly elegance steeped in the romantic traditions of central Europe, Vienna has taken on a whole new lease on life. A fresh, young, innovative generation is moving in, bustling their town into the new Europe with a modern sense of purpose. Since 1990, the gleaming chrome and glass Haas-Haus stands just opposite the Stephansdom (St. Stephan's Cathedral). Shocked old-timers have come to accept it: The rooftop restaurant has a magnificent view of their beloved 850-year-old church.

Old and New

Don't worry, the old faithfuls are there. You can still hear the waltzes of Johann Strauss — only he could describe the muddy brown Danube as blue — and take them all home in a souvenir CD-set. The *Sachertorte* chocolate cake is still the most heavenly accompaniment to your afternoon coffee — traditional creamy Viennese or black *espresso*, if you prefer. The magnificent white Lippizaner horses go through their astonishing paces at the Spanish Riding School. You can ride through town with a plump and jolly bowler-hatted driver in his old-fashioned horse-drawn *Fiaker* cab. He will show you the Habsburgs' imperial palace, aristocratic mansions, and Baroque churches, all shining more brightly than ever in and around the city center. And his brother will race you out to the airport in his limousine. At the Opera House, imagine yourself to be Mozart's Don Giovanni — or one of his beautiful conquests — and then go off to a Heuriger wine-garden for a late-night glass of white wine, and a gloriously sentimental song, on the edge of the Vienna Woods.

For in fact, though it may be unfashionable to admit it, the new dynamic breed of Viennese is very proud of the city's heritage. They have renovated the grand old coffeehouses, for the most part with taste, and the artists, writers, thinkers, and dreamers have now been joined by TV producers and advertising people. And Viennese fashion-designers have taken the time-honored warm woollen *Loden* fabric, still a great defense against the winter winds, to give it a more innovative cut and brighter colors than the traditional olive green jackets, long skirts, and overcoats.

The revered Burgtheater is constantly upsetting its older public with revolutionary productions of uncomfortable authors like Thomas Bernhardt. The great European painters exhibited in the augustly named Kunsthistorisches Museum (Museum of Art History) reflect the grandeur of the Habsburg Empire's royal collections: Brueghel and Rembrandt, Titian and Raphael, Poussin, Velazquez and Dürer. But Vienna is also renowned for its 20th-century masters, Klimt, Schiele, and Kokoschka, beautifully displayed in the Belvedere Palace, and avant-garde artists in the city center's galleries.

East and West

Vienna's historic role as a crossroads of Eastern and Western European civilization has taken on a new significance since the collapse of the Soviet bloc and Austria's entry into the European Union in 1995. A melting pot long before New York, Vienna has always defied a simple national label — just look at the names in the telephone book. As capital of the Habsburg Empire, Vienna was home not only to Slavs and Hungarians, but also to Germans, Spanish, Italians, and even a few Flemish. The Jews, too, such a vital force in pre-1938 Vienna, left their mark on the culture — Sigmund Freud, but also composer Gustav Mahler, playwright Arthur Schnitzler, so many others — and on the slowly awakening conscience of the new generation confronting their parents with that ugly past of the Nazi era. Now, new generations of Poles, Italians, Turks, Croats and every other ethnic group of the former Yugoslavia have again swollen the work force, as well as a sizable group of prosperous and so more leisurely Russians. The language is of course German but, like the cuisine, has that distinctive Viennese touch of incorporating the many ethnic groups that make up the city's population.

Checkmate! Chess enthusiasts mull over a tricky piece position in one of Vienna's many parks.

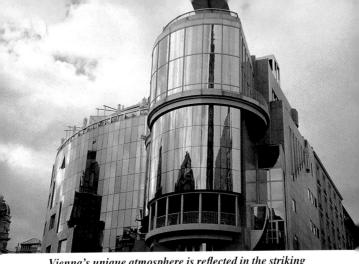

Vienna's unique atmosphere is reflected in the striking contrast between the old and the new.

Much of the town's 18th-century charm and 19th-century pomp has recovered from the onslaught of World War II bombs, postwar building speculation, and modern pollution. Its tree-lined Ringstrasse encircling the Innere Stadt (Inner City, or First District) compares favorably with the airy sweep of Parisian boulevards. In every sense the heart of the city, the Innere Stadt embraces Baroque palaces, elegant shops, coffeehouses, the famous Burgtheater and Staatsoper, and a maze of narrow medieval streets winding around Stephansdom.

Outside the Ringstrasse, the city sprawls through 22 other districts with parks and even farms and vineyards inside the city limits. Vienna is a town with plenty of space to relax in. Its rural setting induces a more easygoing attitude to life than that normally found in modern cities of comparable size.

Not Too *Gemütlich*

The town's relaxed atmosphere often comes as a surprise to visitors. The Viennese still seem to have time for the courtesies of the old days. Shopkeepers like to call regular customers by aristocratic titles that, constitutionally, should have disappeared years ago. Although recent social innovations have been generally popular in Vienna, the people remain profoundly conservative in their values. Politically the Viennese have always been impossible to define. They cheered their Habsburg emperors and then Napoléon. They welcomed the republican experiment after World War I and then hailed Hitler.

And then they found democracy rather nice, too. It seemed conducive to their legendary taste for *Gemütlichkeit*. Roughly translated, *gemütlich* means comfy and cozy — the quality that takes the rough edges off life. It is part of the famous Viennese charm, but a charm also sharpened by undertones of sometimes malicious irony known as *Wiener Schmäh* (Viennese sarcasm). This is much cultivated by the younger generations who know that to thrive in the new century, Vienna must never get too comfy and cozy.

It's easy to hail a taxi in the street, but Fiaker drivers might be in less of a rush.

A BRIEF HISTORY

From earliest times, Vienna was a crossroads for people migrating between eastern and western Europe. The first identifiable inhabitants of the area were Illyrians who sailed up the Danube from the Balkan peninsula. Celts migrating from Gaul around 500 B.C. founded the town of Vindobona ("Shining Field"), which the Romans took over in the first century A.D.

Romans and Barbarians

Sent from Britain to defend the empire's eastern European frontier, Rome's soldiers built their garrison in what is today the Inner City's Hoher Markt. They had their work cut out fending off invasions of the Teutons and Slavs. Emperor Marcus Aurelius personally led the fight against the barbarians, but died in Vindobona of the plague in A.D. 180. A hundred years later, another Roman emperor, Probus, won the gratitude of later generations by developing vineyards on the slopes of the Wienerwald (Vienna Woods). Today, Probusgasse, a street in the heart of the *Heuriger* wine district of Heiligenstadt, honors his initiative.

Christianity arrived in the fourth century, but was powerless against successive waves of barbarian warriors. Attila the Hun advanced on Vienna in 453, but died before implementing plans for its conquest. The Huns were followed over the next 600 years by Goths, Franks, Avars, Slavs, and Magyars, all burning and pillaging their way through the city, even in the face of Charlemagne's pacification efforts at the end of the eighth century. The Frankish king did at least strengthen the hand of the Christians. They had built their first church, Ruprechtskirche, in 740, and were now able to add two others, Maria am Gestade and Peterskirche.

Ruprechtskirche — constructed in the 12th century on the site of an even older house of worship.

Babenberg Rule

Stability came in 1156 when the Babenbergs, Bavarian lords who had succeeded a century and a half earlier in driving out the Magyars, were granted the hereditary duchy of Austria by the Holy Roman Emperor.

The first duke, Heinrich II Jasomirgott, set up his court around what is today the Platz am Hof, giving Vienna its first golden era. Art, trade, and handicrafts thrived, attracting immigrant German merchants and artisans. Vienna became an important stopover for Crusaders. Scottish and Irish monks on their way to Jerusalem founded the monastery of Schottenstift. Babenberg rule brought many new churches, notably the first Stephansdom, as well as several monasteries, elegant residences for the nobility along the broad new thoroughfares, and a fortress on the site of the future Hofburg castle. In 1200, financed with English ransom money paid to liberate King Richard the Lionheart, a ring of fortifications was built around the Innere Stadt, along what is now the Ringstrasse. It was also the great era of the minstrels, start of Vienna's long musical tradition.

On the downside, Friedrich II, known as Friedrich der Streitbare (the Belligerent), disturbed Vienna's hard-earned peace by picking fights with his barons, seducing the burghers' wives, and going off to war at the slightest provocation.

The Habsburgs Settle In

In 1246 the male line of the Babenbergs died out and the country fell to Ottokar II of Bohemia. Ottokar was popular with the Viennese. He made attractive additions to the Stephansdom and started on the Hofburg. The people did not appreciate the efforts of the new German king, Rudolf von Habsburg, to gain

control of the city. They supported Ottokar, but in 1278 Rudolf triumphed.

Vienna's history for centuries thereafter was a constant confrontation between the Habsburgs' visions of grandeur and world conquest and the citizens' taste for the quiet life. Whenever the Habsburgs went about their empire-building, under Maximilian I, Karl V, and Ferdinand I, Vienna was painfully neglected.

An artistic memorial to the plague, Pestsäule is worth a snapshot or two.

The most popular rulers were the ones who preferred to stay home and build things. Rudolf der Stifter (the Founder) created the university in 1365 and turned the Romanesque Stephansdom into the Gothic structure you see today. Friedrich III completed the work and won Rome's approval for Vienna to become a bishopric in 1469. The Viennese showed their appreciation by burying him in the cathedral. As his tomb attests, it was Friedrich who dreamed up the grandiose motto: A.E.I.O.U. - *"Austria Est Imperare Orbi Universo,"* for which an English approximation might be "Austria's Empire Is Our Universe."

The 15th century was not all sweetness and light: In 1421, over 200 Jews were burned alive in their neighborhood around Judenplatz and the rest were driven out of the city. The Hungarian king Matthias Corvinus occupied Vienna from 1485 to 1490. He's remembered for his remark: "Let others wage war while you, happy Austria, arrange marriages. What Mars gives to others, you receive from Venus." The reference was to the Habsburgs' knack of expanding their empire through judicious mating of their innumerable archdukes and archduchesses, a policy that was used to great advantage by Maximilian I (1493–1519).

Picking up where the Goths and the Magyars left off, the Turks under Suleiman the Magnificent staged a crippling eighteen-day siege of Vienna in 1529. The suburbs were devastated, but the Innere Stadt held fast and the infidels were finally forced to retreat.

In the Reformation of the 16th century and the Thirty Years War that followed, the city emerged as a bulwark of the Catholic Church. Having withstood the Muslim Turks, Vienna banned Protestant worship in 1577, and repelled an attack by the Protestant Swedes of Gustavus Adolphus in 1645.

Maria-Theresien-Platz is home to this fishy fountain, one of dozens in Vienna.

Jews were allowed back into town, confined during the 1620s to a ghetto on the riverside marshlands of Leopoldstadt. Emperor Leopold I was the one to usher Vienna into its glorious Baroque era, a feast of architecture and music that scarcely paused to deal with the vicious plague of 1679 and another Turkish siege in 1683. The great soldier and scholar Prince Eugene of Savoy was rewarded for his victory over the Turks with ample funds to build the magnificent and now renowned Belvedere Palace. The Auerspergs, Schwarzenbergs, and Liechtensteins followed suit with palaces on a more modest but equally elegant scale.

Karl VI, pretender to the Spanish throne, returned to Vienna more Spanish than Austrian, bringing with him the strict formality and piety of the Spanish court. His renovation of the 12th-century Abbey Klosterneuburg in Baroque style was an attempt to create an Austrian version of El Escorial. Similarly, the huge Karlskirche was originally intended to emulate St. Peter's in Rome. Vying with Versailles, the Hofburg palace underwent a magnificent expansion which included the building of the Spanish Riding School and the Imperial Library.

Maria Theresa and Napoléon

After this feverish construction that crowned the empire-building efforts of the male Habsburgs, the Viennese were delighted to be able to relax under the maternal eye of Maria Theresa (1740–1780). Pious, warm, and sentimental, this mother of 16 children had an unerring feel for the moods of her capital's citizens. She was an enthusiastic patron of the arts, especially music. She loved to have concerts and operas performed at her newly completed Schönbrunn Palace, which she infinitely preferred to the more austere Hofburg. Her orchestra director was Christoph Gluck. Young Joseph Haydn sang in the Vienna Boys' Choir, and six-year-old Wolfgang Amadeus Mozart won Maria Theresa's heart by asking for the hand of one of her daughters. (In the event, the daughter in question, Marie-Antoinette, was destined to lose her head for somebody else.) In the following years, these three composers — Gluck, Haydn, and Mozart — launched Vienna's reputation as a city of music.

Maria Theresa lulled the Viennese into a false sense of security. Her son Joseph II (1780–1790), very serious-minded and not particularly tactful, shocked them into a reluctant awareness of the revolutionary times that were coming. He rushed through a series of far-reaching reforms, making life easier for peasants, Protestants, and Jews. But the conservative Viennese were not ready. They were startled to see him open up the city by tearing down the wall around the Innere Stadt, and were impressed by the bureaucratic machine he installed to run the empire.

People felt more secure with the cynical and not at all reform-minded Franz II, particularly following the news from France of the execution of Joseph's sister Marie-Antoinette. On seeing the strange tricolor flag hoisted by the new envoy of the French republic, the Viennese promptly tore it to shreds — along with diplomatic relations between Austria and France. They were less bumptious when Napoléon's armies arrived in November 1805 and the French emperor moved into Maria Theresa's beloved Schönbrunn on his way to further glories at Austerlitz.

Once more, the Habsburgs' secret weapon in foreign policy, politically astute marriages, came into play. Now, faced in 1810 with saving what was left of the empire, Emperor Franz did not hesitate to give his daughter Marie-Louise in marriage to his enemy Napoléon. The Viennese did not protest — anything for a quiet life.

The Long 19th Century

The Napoleonic era ended with one of the city's most splendid moments, the Congress of Vienna in 1815, organized by Franz's crafty chancellor Metternich for the postwar carving up of Napoléon's Europe. Franz was happy to leave the diplomatic shenanigans to Metternich while he supervised a non-stop spectacle of banquets, balls, and concerts — all the things the Viennese loved best. Many considered Franz more successful than Metternich. "This Congress does not make progress," said Belgium's Prince de Ligne, "it dances."

For the next 30 years or so the city relaxed for a quiet period of gracious living — dubbed the *Backhendlzeit* (roast chicken era) — an almost democratic time, with the Prater park a favorite outing for royalty and workers alike. And it was time for more music. Beethoven had become the darling of an aristocracy eager to make amends for its shameful neglect of Mozart. But in general the taste was more for the waltzes of Johann Strauss, both father and son.

In 1848 Vienna got caught up in a wave of revolution that spread across Europe in support of national independence and political reform. Ferdinand, the most sweet-natured but also the most dim-witted of Habsburg emperors, exclaimed when he heard that disgruntled citizens were marching on his Hofburg, "Are they allowed to do that?" He fled town before getting an answer. Metternich was forced out of power, and the mob hanged the war minister Theodor Latour from a lamppost before imperial troops brutally re-established order.

Ferdinand abdicated, and his deadly earnest nephew Franz Joseph took over. Grimly aware of his enormous burden, Franz Joseph concentrated throughout his 68-year

A majestic Baroque dome sits atop Karlskirche, the incredible church located near the Ringstrasse.

The students caused a bit of trouble at the Old University, and it was closed in 1848.

reign on defending his family's interests and preserving as much of the empire as possible. Vienna offered him a paradoxically triumphant arena in which to preside over inevitable imperial decline. Prospering from the industrial revolution, the city enthusiastically developed the great Ringstrasse, with imposing residences for capitalism's new aristocracy and expanded residential districts for the burgeoning bourgeoisie.

The World's Fair in 1873 sang the city's praises and people traveled from Europe and America to see the new opera house, concert halls, and theaters. The Austrian empire's cultural achievements were consecrated in monumental form before the empire itself disappeared. Brahms, Bruckner, Mahler, Lehar, and Strauss provided the music. At the Secession Gallery, a group of young artists introduced a new style of art, which came to be known as *Jugendstil* (art nouveau). Only a spoilsport like Sigmund Freud over at the university would suggest that the Viennese examine the depths of their unconscious for the seeds of their darker impulses. They of course paid no attention. As the intellectuals in the coffeehouses clucked disapprovingly, the town waltzed on. A would-be painter named Adolf Hitler left town in disgust at this lack of seriousness, blaming the Jews and Slavs he had encountered in Vienna for the problems of the "true Germans."

The End of the Empire

Having lost his son Rudolf through a suicide in Mayerling, and his wife Elisabeth to an assassin's knife in Geneva, Franz Joseph was stricken but fatalistic when he heard the news that his heir Archduke Franz Ferdinand had been shot in Sarajevo. The world war (1914–1918) that followed ended the Habsburg empire and left Vienna in economic and social ruin.

Vienna lost its hinterland of Czechoslovakia, Hungary, parts of Poland, Romania, and what was then Yugoslavia, all of which had brought it economic prosperity and cultural enrichment.

While the state opera could boast Richard Strauss as its director, and the old creative spirit reemerged in architecturally progressive public housing like the Karl-Marx-Hof, things were not the same. The city suffered from crippling inflation. Politically polarized, vicious street fighting broke out between Communists and fascist supporters of the government of Engelbert Dollfuss.

In 1934 Dollfuss was assassinated by the outlawed Austrian Nazis in the chancellery on Ballhausplatz. His successor, Kurt von Schuschnigg, succeeded in crushing the *putsch* but was forced four years later to yield to Hitler's *Anschluss* (German annexation) of Austria — an idea that originally had the support of both left and right.

On 13 March 1938, Hitler's triumphant drive along the Mariahilferstrasse was cheered by hundreds of thousands of Viennese who saw him as their savior from the chaos of recent years. He proved the opposite for the city's 180,000 Jews. The brutality of the Austrian Nazis and the spite of many local citizens shocked even those who had witnessed their counterparts at work in Germany. The expulsion and extermination of the Jews left a great stain on the city and a gaping hole in the cosmopolitan culture in which the Jews had played such an important role.

In some small measure, the city's spirit survived in World War II. Joseph Bürckel, the Nazi Gauleiter overseeing Vienna, warned Goebbels that it was perhaps better to allow Vienna's satirical cabaret to continue: "One must give more scope to Viennese humor than is usual in the rest of the Reich." All humor had evaporated before the bombardments of 1945, which wrought heavy destruction to almost every major city monument. The cherished Stephansdom, however, was principally the victim of shelling by SS commandos, who then fled with all the fire-fighting equipment.

After the war, Vienna, like Berlin, was divided into four sectors, with the Innere Stadt under the joint four-power administration of the Americans, Russians, British, and French. The penury was countered by stoic good humor but also a vicious black market.

Austria's neutrality, granted in 1955, made Vienna an appropriate host for the International Atomic Energy Agency, the United Nations Industrial Development Organization, and OPEC (Organization of Petroleum Exporting Countries). With the status of a world statesman, Chancellor Bruno Kreisky even gave the city a familiar old whiff of international power-brokering.

Austria joined the European Union in 1995, once more giving Vienna an active role at the heart of Europe. With the entry of an extreme-right party into the government coalition of 2000, the old capital needed all of its time-honored diplomatic talents to deal with the adverse reaction of its European and American allies.

Historical Landmarks

500 B.C. Celts build town of Vindobona.

first century A.D. Romans establish garrison.

fourth–ninth century Barbarian invasions.

740 Ruprechtskirche, earliest known Christian church.

1156–1246 Babenbergs reign as dukes of Vienna, build first Stephansdom cathedral and precursor of Hofburg castle.

1278 Rudolf von Habsburg launches 640-year dynasty.

1365 University of Vienna founded.

1421 Jewish pogrom; 200 burned to death.

1529 First Turkish siege repelled.

1577 Catholic Church bans Reformation Protestants.

17th century Jews return to found Leopoldstadt ghetto.

1683 Second Turkish siege conquered, Prince Eugene of Savoy rewarded with Belvedere Palace.

1740–80 Popular Maria Theresa makes her home in Schönbrunn Palace; Haydn and Mozart make Vienna musical capital.

1780–90 Joseph II's progressive reforms unpopular with conservative Viennese.

1805 Napoléon in Vienna.

1815 Diplomats at Metternich's Congress of Vienna carve up Europe while princes dance.

1848 Short-lived revolt drives Metternich from Vienna. Emperor Ferdinand replaced by Franz Joseph (1848–1916).

1873 World Fair celebrates Vienna's grandeur.

1900 Sigmund Freud writes revolutionary *Interpretation of Dreams*.

1914–18 Defeat in World War I ends Austrian Empire.

1934 Austrian Nazis assassinate Chancellor Dollfuss.

1938 Hitler greeted by cheering Viennese after German annexation (*Anschluss*) of Austria.

1939–45 World War II: Allied bombs devastate city, Stephansdom shelled by German SS.

1955 Austria granted neutrality.

1995 Austria enters European Union.

WHERE TO GO

GETTING AROUND

Vienna makes life relatively easy for the newcomer by packing nearly all its major attractions inside the Innere Stadt (Inner City). This means that places like the Stephansdom (St. Stephen's Cathedral), the Hofburg (Imperial Palace), the Burgtheater (National Theater), Mozart's house, the Staatsoper (State Opera), and the shops on and around Kärtnerstrasse and the Graben are all within walking distance. Even the Kunsthistorisches Museum (Museum of Fine Arts) and Karlskirche are only just outside the Ringstrasse that marks the medieval precincts of the 1st District.

Romantic or just plain footsore, you may like at least once to take a tour in a *Fiaker* horse-drawn carriage. Vienna's answers to Venice's gondolas wait at a number of spots around the Innere Stadt, including Stephansplatz, Albertinaplatz, and Heldenplatz. The best way to view the formidable monuments along the Ringstrasse is by **tram** (*Strassenbahn*). It also provides some 35 other routes to

Ancient and Modern Photo-Ops

Best exterior views of the cathedral are at ground level from the little **Stock-im-Eisen-Platz** leading to the Graben or from the top-floor café in the **Haas Haus** shopping center. *Stock-im-Eisen* (literally, "stick set in iron") refers to the gnarled old trunk into which journeymen locksmiths arriving in medieval Vienna would drive a nail for good luck. The nails are protected now by a glass shield. Haas Haus is an attractively curving structure of glass, chrome and marble built in 1990 by Hans Hollein.

outlying districts, a good cheap way of seeing the neighborhoods on your trip, for instance, to Schönbrunn Palace or a Heuriger wine garden. The **U-Bahn** subway system has five lines, numbered U1 to U6 (U5 has not yet been built). U1 and U3 intersect in the city center at Stephansplatz. The other most conveniently located station is Karlsplatz, which has a good public transport information office, with free maps.

INNERE STADT

Stephansdom

St. Stephan's Cathedral is the heart of Vienna and nobody would thing of starting a city tour anywhere else.

Visit the observation platform at the top of Stephansdom's towering medieval steeple and behold the incredible view.

Whichever way you choose to walk through the Innere Stadt you seem to end up inevitably at the cathedral. For over eight centuries the Stephansdom has watched over Vienna, weathering city fires, Turkish cannonballs, and German and Russian shells.

The steeple, affectionately known as *Steffl* (Stevie), is 137 m (449 ft) high, with an **observation platform** at the top. Count 343 steps to the top, where the view extends northeast to the Czech Republic and southwest to the Semmering Alps.

The main portal takes its name, **Riesentor** (Giant's Gate), from a huge bone found during construction in the 13th century, which was thought to be the shin of a giant drowned in Noah's flood. The bone hung on the door until the Age of Enlightenment, when scientists concluded it was the tibia of a mammoth.

With its Romanesque western façade, Gothic tower, and Baroque altars, the cathedral epitomizes Vienna's grand old genius for harmonious compromise, here managing to seamlessly meld the austerity, dignity, and exuberance of three architectural styles. The Romanesque origins (1240) are strkingly visible in the breathtaking **Heidentürme** (Heathen

One could spend all day exploring the expansive interior of Stephansdom.

Towers) and statuary depicting, among others, a griffin and Samson fighting a lion. Above the entrance are Jesus, the Apostles, and a veritable menagerie of dragons, lions, reptiles, and birds representing evil spirits to be exorcised by the sanctity of the church.

The mainly Gothic structure we see today was built in the 14th and 15th centuries. To support their petition to have Vienna made a bishopric, the Habsburgs hoped to impress the Pope by adding a second tower. But the city fathers preferred to spend the money on strengthening city fortifications against the Turks and Protestants. The north tower was never properly completed, just topped off in 1578 with a nicely frivolous Renaissance cupola. Part of the Stephansdom's charm derives from the asymmetry of its steeple set to one side.

> **The Viennese greet each other with a "Servus!" or "Grüss Gott!" but never utter the unacceptably German "Tschüss" when parting ways.**

From atop the North Tower (by elevator), you have a fine view of the city. The 20-ton **Pummerin bell** is a recast version of the one made from the bronze of Turkish cannons captured after the 1683 siege, but destroyed in the wartime fire of 1945. It is rung only on ceremonial occasions such as New Year's Eve.

Inside the church in the center aisle is the charming carved Gothic **pulpit** of Master Anton Pilgram. At the head of the spiral staircase the sculptor has placed the figures of Augustine, Gregory, Jerome, and Ambrose, Fathers of the Church — and added a sculpture of himself looking through a window under the staircase. No shrinking violent, Pilgram pops up again at the foot of the elaborate stone organ-base he built in the north aisle.

Left of the high altar is the carved wooden **Wiener Neustädter Altar.** To the right is the marble **tomb** of

Emperor Friedrich III (died 1493), honored by the Viennese for having the city made a bishopric, and for inventing the *Semmel,* the little bread roll you get with every meal.

Around Stephansdom

To relax after the cathedral, walk up Rotenturmstrasse to one of the outdoor cafés on **Lugeck,** a pleasant little square where they used to hang burglars some 300 years ago. From there, wander over to the Fleischmarkt; at number 11 you'll find the oldest tavern in Vienna, the **Griechenbeisl** (1490), frequented by Mozart, Beethoven, Schubert, and Strauss, and where Mark Twain scribbled his short story, "The $1,000,000 Bank-Note."

Around the corner on Grashofgasse, cross the courtyard of the 17th-century **Heiligenkreuzerhof** abbey to the **Basiliskenhaus** (Schönlaterngasse 7), steeped in medieval superstition. Here a basilisk — half rooster, half lizard — was said to have breathed its poisonous fumes into the drinking water, until one day a baker's apprentice held up a mirror to the monster and scared it to death.

It is a stone's throw over to the **Alte Universität** (Old University, 1365), where young Franz Schubert lived as a member of the Vienna Boys' Choir. The Alte Universität was closed down after student demonstrations in 1848 against the autocratic regime of Metternich. The authorities move the hotheads out of the Innere Stadt to academies in the outer districts until a new university was opened in 1884, safely on the outer edge of the Ring.

On the Bäckerstrasse, the Baroque house of the old Schmauswaberl restaurant (number 16) served students cheap meals with leftovers from the Hofburg kitchens. The French lady of letters Madame de Staël lived at the Palais Seilern, and across the street (at number 7) is a beautiful ivy-covered arcaded Renaissance courtyard.

Figarohaus on Domgasse is where Mozart composed
"The Marriage of Figaro" — beneath this very ceiling!

Cut across the busy Wollzeile to Domgasse 5, where, from 1784 to 1787 Wolfgang Amadeus Mozart lived in the **Figarohaus.** In this house, now a museum, Mozart wrote eleven piano concertos, one horn concerto, two quintets, four quartets, three trios, three piano sonatas, two violin sonatas, and the opera *The Marriage of Figaro.* It is a thrill for music lovers to stand in the very room where Mozart received a respectful visit from Joseph Haydn and where the young Ludwig van Beethoven applied for music lessons. These were the great days. Four years later, around the corner in musty Rauhensteingasse, Mozart struggled to finish *The Magic Flute* and a Requiem before his time ran out. He died a pauper, his coffin assigned to an anonymous grave.

Cheer up with a stroll through the **Fähnrichshof** at the corner of Blutgasse and Singerstrasse. This charming com-

plex of artists' studios, galleries, boutiques, apartments, and gardens is a triumph of urban renovation from the total ruin left by World War II bombs. The nearby **Franziskanerplatz** presents a fine Baroque ensemble — 18th-century fountain with a statue of Moses by Johann Martin Fischer, elegant Franziskanerkirche, and the Kleines Café tastefully remodelled by Hermann Czech.

Kärntnerstrasse

Kärntnerstrasse was once the city's main north–south thoroughfare, continuing on through Carinthia (Kärnten) to Trieste on the Adriatic. It has always been the central artery of Viennese social life, perhaps because it so neatly joins the sacred and the profane — the Stephansdom at one end and the Staatsoper at the other.

Go down Moses — way down to Franziskanerplatz. Let my people go to this busy district.

The street, which has been transformed to a traffic-free pedestrian zone, boasts many of Vienna's smartest shops. Most are modern, but the Lobmeyr shop (number 26) dates back to 1823 and now houses a **glassware museum.** The open-air cafés are an innovation in a town not hitherto noted for its street life. The Gothic **Malteserkirche** (number 37) was founded by the Crusading Order of Maltese Knights.

Just off Kärntnerstrasse, on Neuer Markt, is the **Kaisergruft,** a 17th-century imperial burial vault beneath the church of the Capuchin Friars (Kapuzinerkirche). Among the tombs and sarcophagi of some 140 Habsburgs, note the double casket of Maria Theresa and her husband, François de Lorraine. The most recent burial was in 1989, of Zita, wife of the last Habsburg emperor, Karl I (who abdicated in 1918 and is buried in Madeira).

> Except in restaurants requiring a reservation, customers rarely have to wait to be seated. You can sit wherever you want.

Almost equally venerable, certainly more appetizing, is the monumental **Hotel Sacher,** on another side-street, Philharmonikerstrasse. This opulent piece of Neo-Classical architecture is world-famous for its *Sachertorte* chocolate cake (see page 92).

On Albertinaplatz is the bleak **Monument Against War and Fascism** (1991) by Alfred Hrdlicka. Facing the stone gate symbolizing totalitarian force is the controversial bronze sculpture of a kneeling figure, recalling the humiliation of Jews forced by the Nazi regime to scrub pavements with a tooth brush. The monument has been contested both by Jews and anti-Semites.

The Graben

The **Graben** is the center, with the adjacent Kohlmarkt and Dorotheergasse, of the town's most fashionable shops and coffeehouses. Till the end of the Habsburgs, it was equally infamous for its "Graben nymphs," as the local ladies of the night were known.

The board street is now a pedestrian zone, dominated by the startling, bulbous-shaped monument to the town's deliverance from the plague in 1679. The **Pestsäule** (Plague

Column) combines humility before God and gruesome fascination with the disease itself. A more joyous celebration of faith, just off the Graben, is the **Peterskirche** (St. Peter's Church), designed in 1702 by Gabriele Montani and completed by Johann Lukas von Hildebrandt. The exterior embraces the graceful oval of its nave, its rows of pews curving outwards, each decorated with three carved angels' heads. It displays the genius of Viennese Baroque for marrying the sumptuous to the intimate.

In and Around the Jewish Quarter

The new **Jüdisches Museum** (Jewish Museum) is at Dorotheergasse 11 (see page 60), but the old **Jewish quarter,** still in large part a garment district, lies north of the Graben. Its medieval center was **Judenplatz** (Jews' Square) until the pogrom of 1421 (see page 15), when the synagogue was dismantled and its stones carted off to build an extension to the

---

A Song for Richard

During the Crusade of 1191, the brave but cheeky English king Richard the Lion-Heart enraged Leopold V von Babenberg by replacing the Austrian flag in Acre, Palestine, with the English one. Worse than that, he prevented the Austrians from sharing in the booty. But, on his way home, though dressed as a peasant, Richard was recognized and thrown into the darkest dungeon of Dürnstein. He languished there for several years until the faithful minstrel Blondel came looking for him, singing a song known only to the king and himself. Richard revealed his place of imprisonment by joining in the chorus. His ransom, 23,000 kilos of silver, was enough to finance the Holy Roman Empire's expedition to Sicily and to build a new Ring Wall around Vienna.

The elaborate church of St. Peter (Peterskirche) was not built in a day — it took thirty years to construct.

Alte Universität. Today, a commemorative monument is being built facing a statue of the great German humanist Gottfried Ephraim Lessing.

The one **synagogue** (out of the city's 24) that survived the Nazis' 1938 Kristallnacht pogrom is at Seitenstettengasse 4, next to a kosher restaurant. With its Jewish community center, it stands behind a protective block of apartment buildings beside the unusual **Kornhäuselturm** (1827), studio and home of architect Josef Kornhäusel. Inside is a drawbridge he pulled up whenever he wanted to shut himself off from his quarrelsome wife.

Nearby Judengasse leads to the city's most ancient church, the ivy-covered Romanesque **Ruprechtskirche** (1161).

Go west to Salvatorgasse, past the superb porch of the **Salvatorkapelle,** a happy marriage of Italian Renaissance and Austrian late-Gothic sculpture. Beyond it is the slender 14th-century Gothic, the church of **Maria am Gestade** ("Mary on the banks"), originally overlooking the Danube. Notice its delicate tower, the canopied porch, and remains of Gothic stained glass in the choir.

Roman Vienna

Ruprechtskirche is near the northeast corner of the original Roman settlement, Vindobona — bounded by Rotenturmstrasse to the east, Salzgries to the north, Tiefer Graben to the west, and Naglergasse and Graben to the south. Marc Aurel-Strasse, named after the Roman emperor who died in A.D. 180, takes you from the

> **Signs:**
> *Eingang–entrance*
> *Ausgang–exit*
> *Eintritt frei–admission free*

Ruprechtskirche to the **Hoher Markt,** once Vindobona's forum. A little museum (at number 2) shows remains of two Roman houses laid bare by a 1945 bombardment. At the eastern end of the square is a gem of high Viennese kitsch, the **Ankeruhr,** an animated clock built in 1911 by a local insurance company. Charlemagne, Prince Eugene, Maria Theresa, Joseph Haydn, and others perform their act at midday.

Platz am Hof

Walk back across the Judenplatz to the spacious **Platz am Hof,** the largest square in the old part of the city. The Babenberg dukes, predecessors of the Habsburgs, built their fortress (on the site of number 7) in about 1150. It was both military stronghold and a palace for festivities such as the rollicking state reception in 1165 for German Emperor Friedrich Barbarossa.

The **Mariensäule** (column to Mary) was erected in 1667 to celebrate victory over Sweden's armies in the Thirty Years' War. It was on a lamp-post in the middle of this square that the revolutionaries of 1848 hanged War Minister Theodor Latour. At the **Am Hof church,** a Baroque re-working of a late-Gothic structure, the end of the Holy Roman Empire, said by some to be neither Holy nor Roman nor an Empire, was pro-claimed with fanfare in 1806.

Around Herrengasse

In Bognergasse, notice the pretty Jugendstil façade of the **Engel-Apotheke** (1907) before returning to medieval Vienna through narrow cob-ble-stoned Naglergasse. This leads to the **Freyung**

A local insurance company built Ankeruhr, guaranteeing the clock's daily show.

triangle, flanked by the Palais Harrach (where Joseph Haydn's mother was the family cook) and the **Schottenkirche** (Church of the Scots), founded by Scottish and Irish Benedictine monks in the 12th century.

South of the Freyung is Herrengasse, the Innere Stadt's main eastbound traffic artery, lined with imposing Baroque and Neo-Baroque palaces. Now government offices or embassies, these buildings belonged to Vienna's great

Austrian, Hungarian, Italian, and Czech families — Kinsky, Modena, Wilczek, Pallavicini, and Batthyaninow.

Here, too, is the 18th-century **Palais Ferstel**, incorporating an elegant shopping arcade, Freyung Passage, and the restored **Café Central,** Vienna's leading coffeehouse before World War I (see page 95). Upstairs, a restaurant occupies the gilded premises of the old stock exchange.

Herrengasse leads to Michaelerplatz and the Hofburg (see pages 40–41). Once the imperial parish church, **Michaelerkirche** is a hybrid mixture of Romanesque, Gothic, and Baroque. At number 5 is the architecturally revolutionary **Looshaus,** now a bank. Built by Adolf Loos, its starkly functional use of fine materials shocked many in 1910. Emperor

Benedictine monks founded the Schottenkirche, which does not feature the traditional Viennese architecture.

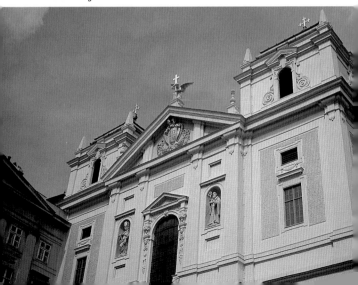

Franz Joseph so hated its "outrageously naked" façade that he stopped using the Hofburg's Michaelertor exit.

Ringstrasse

Before tackling the Hofburg, take a walk (or tram ride) around the Ringstrasse, the single urban achievement of Franz Joseph. This boulevard encircling the Innere Stadt was mapped out in the 1860s along the route of the old city walls. Inspired by what the emperor had seen on a visit to Paris, the project captured

> **Fuel types for cars/trucks:**
> *Bleifrei*–unleaded
> *Normal*–regular
> *Super*–premium
> *Diesel*–diesel

the energetic optimism of the times. The Neo-Classical buildings bring together all the great architectural styles of Europe's past.

Start west of the Schottenring, at the Votivkirche, a Neo-Gothic church built after Franz Joseph survived an assassination attempt in 1853. Next to it are the University and **Rathaus** (Town Hall). Proceed along the Innere Stadt side, past the imposing **Burgtheater** (see page 84), a high temple of German theater. Beyond is the lovely **Volksgarten.** Its cafés and concerts carry on a tradition that began with the café music of the Strauss family.

Opposite, bypass the temple-like Parliament, built by Theophil Hansen after a long stay in Athens, and save till later the Naturhistorisches and Kunsthistorisches museums (see pages 52–57), and the Neue Burg (see page 45). The **Burggarten,** the Hofburg's park, leads to the **Staatsoper** (State Opera). The original opera house, inaugurated in 1869, was greeted with a rain of criticism that drove one of the architects, Edward van der Nüll, to suicide. It was almost completely destroyed in the 1945 bombardments. The new house captures the original's Neo-Classical spirit.

On Karlsplatz, the huge **Karlskirche** is the most important of the city's Baroque churches. It was built by Fischer von Erlach for Karl VI, fulfilling an oath made by the emperor during the plague of 1713. Sunset offers a spectacular view of the big dome across the Karlsplatz.

The cool, sober interior has a subdued marble décor and spacious oval ground plan similar to that of the Peterskirche (see page 32). The oval dome's ceiling **frescoes** are by Johann Michael Rottmayr, the trompe-l'oeil by Gaetano Fanti. Notice, too, Naiel Gran's lovely painting of **St. Elisabeth** in the main chapel on the right.

Public phones now take either coins or telephone card (*Telefonwertkarte*) often both in the same machine.

In front of the church, a massive **Henry Moore sculpture** provides a striking contrast. Also on Karlsplatz is Otto Wagner's **Stadtbahn Pavilion** (Municipal Railway Pavilion) with its graceful green, gold, and white motif of sunflowers and tulips. In the 1900s, Wagner led Viennese architecture away from its academic tradition through decorative *Jugendstil* into functional modernism.

His movement is celebrated at the corner of Friedrichstrasse with the **Secession building** (1897–1898) of his student Joseph Olbrich. It accommodated a new generation of artists, led by Gustav Klimt, who in 1897 broke away from the conservative academies. An inscription above the door proclaims: *"Der Zeit ihre Kunst, der Kunst ihre Freiheit."* ("To the Age, its own Art; to Art, its own Freedom.") The dome of gilded iron laurel leaves symbolizes the interdependence of art and nature. Today, it exhibits works by contemporary artists. In the basement is Gustav

The stylistic hodgepodge of Vienna's many churches keeps them interesting — you never know what to expect!

Contemporary sculpture and an ancient church show the fusion of history and modernity that is Vienna.

Klimt's magnificent **Beethoven Frieze,** created for a Secession exhibition in 1902.

The largest collection of Klimt's paintings — along with works of his contemporaries Schiele and Kokoschka — can be seen in the Austrian Gallery in the Upper Belvedere (see page 51).

PALACES

 ### Hofburg

Defeat in war took away the Habsburgs, but not the palaces. They remain to warm the cockles of Vienna's imperial heart.

Most imposing is the Hofburg, home of Austria's rulers since the 13th century. It covers the southwest corner of the Innere Stadt in a confusing but awe-inspiring sprawl reminiscent of the empire itself.

The vast palace went through five major stages of construction over six centuries, and at the end there was still a large unfinished section. Start at the Hofburg's beginning, right in the middle at the **Schweizerhof,** named after the Swiss Guard once housed there. Here King Ottokar of Bohemia built a fortress in 1275–1276 to resist Rudolf von Habsburg. Victorious Rudolf moved in and strengthened the fortifications to keep the unruly Viennese out. By the Schweizertor archway are the pulleys for the chains of the drawbridge. But Rudolf's son, Albrecht I, preferred the safety of Leopoldsberg in the Vienna Woods. For 250 years, the fortress was used only for meetings with visiting kings and other ceremonial occasions. The **Burgkapelle** (Castle Chapel), in the northern corner of the Schweizerhof, was built in 1449. Originally Gothic, it was redone in Baroque style and then partially restored to its original form in 1802. The Wiener Sängerknaben (Vienna Boys' Choir) sing Mass here on Sundays and public holidays (except during summer holidays) at 9:15am.

In 1533, four years after the Turks were driven off, Ferdinand I felt safe enough to settle in the Hofburg, bringing his barons and bureaucrats to make their homes in nearby Herrengasse and Wallnerstrasse. He built the **Stallburg** in 1565 (outside the main Hofburg complex on Reitschulgasse) as a home for his son Archduke Maximilian. It was subsequently turned into stables for the horses of the Spanish Riding School. With its fine three-story arcaded courtyard, the Stallburg is the most important Renaissance building in Vienna.

Also in Renaissance style is Rudolf II's **Amalienburg** (1611), with a pleasant trapezoid-shaped courtyard. Maria Theresa redecorated it as part of her futile effort to make the Hofburg into a cozy home, and Elisabeth, wife of Franz Joseph, lived here when she was in Vienna.

For a while, the Habsburgs neglected Vienna in favor of Prague, but in the 17th century they returned and tried to make the Hofburg into a kind of Versailles. Leopold I launched the city's Baroque era with his **Leopoldinischer Trakt** (Leopold Wing) — a residence in keeping with the Habsburgs' role as a world power. (Today the Leopoldinis-

Jugendstil-Vienna around 1900

In Austria, *Jugendstil* caught the imagination of the art world, and the result was the foundation of the Secession by a group of renegade artists from the Academy in 1897. The central figure of the Secession was Gustav Klimt (1862–1918), whose erotic, fairytale-like painting and themes came to embody *Jugendstil* for many. One of the key tenets for artists like Klimt and Koloman Moser, and architects Otto Wagner and Josef Hoffmann, was the linking of function and aesthetic.

Klimt's decorative elegance was a particular source of inspiration for Egon Schiele (1890–1918), whose linearity and subtlety reveals the strong influence of the *Jugendstil* movement. Schiele, however, emphasized expression over decoration, concentrating on the human figure with an acute eroticism that was less decorative than Klimt's. Evocation of intense feeling through colors and lines was of equal importance to Oskar Kokoschka (1886–1980), a leading exponent of Expressionism.

The Schweizerhof is sometimes the location of choice for the Viennese elite to hold their private affairs.

cher Trakt is the home of the Austrian president, a purely ceremonial post.) Karl VI promoted the Habsburgs' new self-confidence with the **Reichskanzlei** (Imperial Chancellery), where Franz Joseph later had his apartments, the **Hofbibliothek** (the Court Library, now the National Library), and the Winterreitschule (Winter — or Spanish — Riding School).

It was no longer necessary to call on foreign talent. Johann Bernhard Fischer von Erlach, his son Joseph Emmanuel, and Johann Lukas von Hildebrandt were among the outstanding court architects of the time. **Josefsplatz,** a marvelously harmonious Baroque square, was designed by the Fischer von Erlachs (who built the National Library) and Jean-Nicolas Jadot. Jadot designed the adjoining **Redoutensaal,** now beautifully restored after a devastating fire in 1992. The library's **Prunksaal** (Great Hall) is one of the finest Baroque interiors in the world.

Just off the Josefsplatz is the Habsburgs' wedding church, **Augustinerkirche.** The façade of this Gothic and Baroque structure matches the library and Redoutensaal. It was here that Maria Theresa married François of Lorraine in 1736, Marie-Louise married Napoléon (in absentia) in 1810, and Franz Joseph married Elisabeth in 1854. Though the Habsburgs' burial church is the Kapuzinerkirche over on

A horse-drawn Fiaker tour is a romantic way to explore Vienna, although the kids are sure to like it too!

Neuer Markt (see page 30), the heart of the deceased was buried in the Augustiner crypt.

At the end of the 19th century, Franz Joseph embarked on building a gigantic Kaiser Forum (Emperor Forum). This was to have embraced the vast **Heldenplatz** (Heroes' Square) with two crescent-shaped arms, the whole extending through triumphal arches to the Naturhistorisches and Kunsthistorisches museums. Only the first of the two crescents, the **Neue Burg** was built before the empire collapsed. Today, it houses a congress center, several museums, and reading rooms for the National Library (open to all on day passes).

The Habsburgs could really light up a room with these ornate crystal chandeliers.

To sense the human scale of the Habsburgs' gigantic enterprise, take the 45-minute guided tour of the **imperial apartments** (Kaiserappartements). Coming from the Michaelerplatz, entrance is left of the Hofburg rotunda. You will see splendid Gobelin tapestries; a smoking room for the emperor's fellow officers; enormous Rococo stoves needed to heat the place; a crystal chandelier weighing half a ton; Franz Joseph's austere bedroom with iron military camp-bed; and Elisabeth's rooms and gymnasium for daily exercises on wall-bars and climbing ropes to keep her wasp-waisted figure.

☞ Spanish Riding School

The magnificent Baroque hall of the **Spanish Riding School** is worth visiting on architectural grounds alone. The Lipizzaner horses perform in its elegant arena throughout the year, except in January, February, July, and August.

Tickets must be booked at least six months in advance (write to Spanische Reitschule, Hofburg, A - 1010 Vienna). A cheaper option is to watch the horses train. Morning exercises are held 10am to noon Tuesday to Saturday (except in midwinter, July, and August). Tickets are sold from 8:30am at the entrance, Josefsplatz, Gate 2 (reservations cannot be made).

The Lipizzaner, originally a Spanish breed, were raised at Lipica in Slovenia, not far from Trieste; since 1920 the tradi-

> **Kissing a lady's hand has been replaced by just stating the intention: "*Küss die Hand, gnädige Frau.*"**

tion has been carried on in the Styrian town of Piber. By methods that have not changed since the 17th century, the horses are trained to walk and dance with a delicacy that many ballet dancers would envy. They perform classical figures to the music of the polka, gavotte, quadrille — and the Viennese waltz.

Discover another world in another age as these shining white horses with gold ribbons tied into their plaited manes and tails are led in by equerries wearing cocked hats, brown tailcoats edged with black silk, white buckskin breeches, sabers, and riding boots. Custom demands that gentlemen take their hats off when the equerries enter. The spectacle more than merits the gesture.

☞ Schönbrunn

Affairs of state were not something Maria Theresa ran away from, but she did prefer to handle them in the more

The elegant Lipizzaner stallions practice (and perform) their groovy moves at the Spanish Riding School.

gemütlich setting of Schönbrunn (accessible by tram and subway). As soon as she was settled on the throne in 1740, she moved into the palace Leopold I built as a summer residence and which her father, Karl VI, had used as a lodge for pheasant hunts.

If the Hofburg is the oversized expression of a dynasty that outgrew itself, Schönbrunn is the smiling, serene expression of the personality of one woman, imperial nonetheless. Finding Fischer von Erlach's various ideas for a "Super Versailles" too pompous, Maria Theresa brought in her favorite architect, Nikolaus Pacassi. He made Schönbrunn an imposing edifice with warm and decorative Rococo interiors — a symbol of Maria Theresa's "idyllic absolutism."

To appreciate Schönbrunn's tendency to pleasure rather than imperial pomp, visit the **gardens** first. With the exception of the Kammergarten (Chamber Garden) and Kronprinzengarten (Crown Prince Garden) immediately left and right of the palace, the park has always been open to the public. Maria Theresa liked to have her Viennese around her. The park, laid out in classical French manner, is dominated by the **Gloriette,** a Neo-Classical colonnade perched on the crest of a hill. It is difficult to say which view is prettier — the graceful silhouette of the Gloriette against a sunset viewed from the palace, or a bright morning view from the Gloriette over the whole of Vienna to the north and the Wienerwald to the south.

The Neo-Classical lines of Gloriette at Schönbrunn speak volumes with their simplicity and precision.

On the way to the Gloriette you will pass the Neptune Fountain and countless other statues of ancient mythology. East of the Neptune Fountain are the half-buried artificial **"Roman ruins,"** built by von Hohenberg in 1778, complete with fragmented Corinthian columns, friezes, and archways. Nearby is the Schöner Brunnen (Beautiful Spring), discovered by Emperor Matthias around 1615, from which the palace took its name. West of Neptune is a little

> *Bier* or *Wein* is served practically everywhere — even in American fast food chains.

zoo, established in 1752 by François de Lorraine, the consort of Maria Theresa, a topiary maze, and a Tyrolean Garden (with a café).

Crossing the courtyard to the palace's front entrance, you'll see on the right the **Schlosstheater,** now the site of summer chamber opera performances. In 1908, Franz Joseph's 60th anniversary as emperor was celebrated here with a ballet that included 43 Habsburg archdukes and archduchesses, aged 3 to 18.

A guided tour of the **palace** (in English) shows some of the sumptuous coziness enjoyed by Maria Theresa and her successors: her breakfast room, decorated with the needlework of the empress and her myriad daughters; the **Spiegelsaal** (Hall of Mirrors), in which the young Mozart gave his first royal recital; the **Chinesisches Rundkabinett** (Chinese Round Room), also known as Maria Theresa's Konspirationstafelstube (roughly: "top secret dining room"). For her secret consultations, a table rose from the floor with a completely prepared dinner so that no servants would be present during the conversation. Guests used the **billiard room** while awaiting an audience with Franz Joseph. He, too, preferred Schönbrunn to the Hofburg and kept his mistress, actress Katharina Schratt, in a villa in the neighboring district of Hietzing. Also on view is the bedroom where he died on 30 November 1916, at the age of 86.

The stately and the human are poignantly juxtaposed in the opulence of the ballrooms and dining rooms and the intimacy of the living quarters. The **Napoléon Room** (originally Maria Theresa's bedroom) was used by the French emperor on his way to victory at Austerlitz and by his son, the Duke of Reichstadt, in his last sad years. It is both pathetic and awesome to sense Napoléon's presence in a room that now contains his son's death mask and stuffed pet bird. Down the hall, the last Habsburg abdicated at the end of World War I and Kennedy and Khrushchev met for dinner at the height of the Cold War. In the adjoining **Wagenburg museum,** you can see an impressive collection of coaches used by the imperial court, including the gilded coronation car of Karl VI.

> Satisfy the Viennese passion for gossip with new tittle-tattle about Buckingham Palace or the White House.

☞ Belvedere

The summer palace of Prince Eugene of Savoy is regarded as the finest flower of Vienna's Baroque residential architecture. Though close to the Innere Stadt, in the Third District, the palace is an enchanted world apart with its allegorical sculptures, fountains, waterfalls, ponds, and gardens.

The **Unteres** (Lower) **Belvedere** was built by Johann Lukas von Hildebrandt in 1714–1716, and served as Prince Eugene's summer residence. (His winter palace is another jewel now brightening the lives of bureaucrats in the Finance Ministry on Himmelpfortgasse.) The palace was acquired by Maria Theresa after the prince's death, and was used by various members of the Habsburg dynasty, including Archduke Franz Ferdinand, whose assassination at Sarajevo in 1914 sparked World War I. Today

the Lower Belvedere houses the Museum of Austrian Baroque Art (see page 57), while the palace's **Orangerie** is home to the Museum of Medieval Austrian Art (see page 58).

Prince Eugene held banquets and other festivities in the **Oberes** (or Upper) **Belvedere,** completed in 1723. In 1955, the four victorious powers of World War II met here to sign the treaty for Austria's independence as a neutral country. Today the Upper Belvedere houses the Austrian Gallery of 19th- and 20th-century art (see page 58). Its **terrace** offers a splendid panoramic view of the city skyline, remarkably little changed since Bellotto-

How gemütlich can it be for Viennese royalty in the Belvedere Palace?

Canaletto painted it in 1760. For your walk through the gardens, start at the Upper Belvedere, entrance Prinz-Eugen-Strasse 27. The sunset view is a pure delight.

MUSEUMS

Vienna has over 120 museums, ranging from the Kunsthistorisches Museum and the Albertina to the Circus and Clown Museum and Firefighting Museum. The tourist information office's free *Museums* brochure provides a comprehensive list. Many of these museums can be visited for

free or at reduced rates with the Vienna Card, available from the tourist information office and other locations. (See BUDGETING FOR YOUR TRIP in the *Handy Travel Tips* section, page 100.)

Kunsthistorisches Museum

Maria-Theresien-Platz (wheelchair access Burgring 5). Closed Monday. Open 10am–6pm, Thursday till 9pm. U-Bahn 2: Babenbergerstrasse, Tram D, J, 1, 2: Burgring.

Kunsthistorisches might be tough to say, but spending the day there will be a breeze.

If the Kunsthistorisches Museum (Museum of Fine Arts) is less well known than the Louvre or the Prado, it may just be that the name is such a mouthful. The collection is, quite simply, magnificent. Benefiting from the cultural diversity of the Habsburg empire, it in fact encompasses a much broader spectrum of Western European art than its better known counterparts.

In such a vast collection, we recommend newcomers to concentrate on a few of the masterpieces. Start with the Gallery of Paintings (Gemäldegalerie) on the first floor — European art from the 16th to 18th centuries, arranged by national school. Dutch, Flemish, German, and English works are in the east wing, left of the main entrance, and Italian, Spanish, and French works in the west wing, to the right.

Gallery of Paintings First Floor, East Wing

The list below represents key works by some of the greatest Dutch, Flemish, and German pre-modern masters.

Pieter Brueghel the Elder (c. 1525–1569). An entire room comprising nearly half of the Flemish artist's total output, including popular peasant themes such as *Children's Games* and *Peasant Wedding*, and biblical subjects such as *Christ Carrying the Cross* and *Building the Tower of Babel*.

Albrecht Dürer (1471–1528). Six of the great German master's works are on display, including the celebrated *Martyrdom of 10,000 Christians*. The artist brings the same dignity to his worldly *Portrait of Emperor Maximilian I* as to his intensely spiritual *The Holy Trinity Surrounded by All Saints*.

Lucas Cranach the Elder (1472–1553). Notice his splendid painting of an almost provocatively serene Judith holding the head of the Assyrian general Holofernes, whom she has just decapitated.

Hans Holbein the Younger (1497–1543). Outstanding tight-lipped portrait of Henry VIII's third wife, *Jane Seymour*.

Anthony Van Dyck (1599–1641). The Flemish master's dramatic *Capture of Samson* shows a talent beyond his more familiar portraits.

Peter Paul Rubens (1577–1640). Besides the vast ceremonial pictures in the extensive Rubens selection, enjoy the more intimate portrait of his fat and sassy second wife Hélène Fourment — titled *The Little Fur Coat*. Rubens' *Self-Portrait* is also on display.

Rembrandt (1606–1669). The collection includes two superb self-portraits and a portrait of the artist's mother.

Jan Vermeer (1632–1675). The celebrated *Allegory of Painting* shows the Dutch artist painting his Muse as a shy young lady.

Thomas Gainsborough (1727–1788). The evocative *Suffolk Landscape* is enough to make even the most unpatriotic Englishman homesick.

Jacob van Ruisdael (1628–1682). *Big Forest* serves as a soothing finale to the museum's Northern European paintings.

Gallery of Paintings First Floor, West Wing

This section is devoted primarily to Italian masters.

Ludwig van Beethoven (1770–1827)

Beethoven came to Vienna at the age of 22 to take lessons with Haydn. He soon established a reputation for himself with his early piano trios and sonatas, and the Viennese aristocracy were quick to take this new genius into their homes. These were his happiest years in Vienna. He fell in love with one after another of the three Brunswick daughters. It was during this period that he wrote his "Pathétique" and "Moonlight" sonatas.

By 1800, deafness had set in. He moved to Heiligenstadt to be near the park's reputed waters in the desperate hope that he might find a cure. It was at Probusgasse 6, in 1802, that he wrote in his famous Heiligenstadt Testament: "You are unjust, you who believe me hostile, obstinate and a misanthrope, or at least said I was. In fact you didn't know the secret reasons for the character traits you attributed to me. But could I tell you: 'Speak louder, shout, I am deaf'?"

And yet less than a year after writing this, he finished his Second Symphony, as joyous a work as any he ever wrote.

It is said that his death, after long illness, came in the middle of a tremendous rainstorm, with the great man shaking his fist at the lightning, enraged that he could not hear the thunder.

Giorgione (c. 1476–1510). The *Three Philosophers* is one of the few authenticated Giorgiones in existence.

Raphael (1483–1520). Inspired by Leonardo da Vinci, *Madonna Amid Greenery* is a High Renaissance masterpiece depicting the pyramid of Mary, Jesus, and John.

Titian (c. 1487–1576). The Venetian painter is represented by the majestic *Ecce Homo* of Christ before Pontius Pilate, as well as by two lovely madonnas.

Paolo Veronese (c. 1528–1588). The Venetian master is represented by his biblical painting of the *Healing of the Haemophiliac.*

This Durer portrait is part of the magnificent collection housed in the museum.

Jacopo Tintoretto (1518–1594). *Susanna in Her Bath* shows a delightfully wistful woman (from the Biblical Apocrypha) performing her absolutions.

Caravaggio (1571–1610). His *Rosary Madonna* and *David with Goliath's Head* are full of characteristic vigor and immediacy.

Giovanni Battista Tiepolo (1696–1770). A magnificent portrayal of Roman history in *The Death of Brutus* and *Hannibal Recognizes the Head of his Brother*.

Velázquez (1599–1660). His famous paintings of the Spanish court include the splendid *Infanta Margarita Teresa* in her blue dress, *King Philip IV,* and *Queen Isabella*.

"Take that, you nasty centaur, you." Antonio Canova's marble sculpture is grandiose in stature.

Bernardo Bellotto (1721–1780). The artist followed his uncle Canaletto's example — he even used the same name at times — producing panoramic views for the great courts of Europe. Those of Vienna include the Freyung, the Neue Markt, and the *City Seen from the Belvedere*.

Mezzanine Galleries

The lower floor of the museum contains an impressive collection of ancient Egyptian, Greek, and Roman art, as well as the **Sculpture and Applied Arts Collection,** whose prized possession is Benvenuto Cellini's famous gold-enameled **salt cellar** made for King François I of France. The highlight of the **Classical Antiquities Collection** is the exquisite *Gemma Augustea,* a first-century onyx cameo. The **Egyptian/Oriental Collection** contains, among other treasures, the burial chamber of Prince Kaninisut. The top floor of the museum holds the **Secondary Gallery** of paintings and the **Numismatic Collection.**

Naturhistorisches Museum

Maria-Theresien-Platz (facing Kunsthistorisches Museum), open 9am–6pm, closed Tuesday. U-Bahn 2, 3: Volkstheater, Tram D, J, 1, 2: Dr. Karl-Renner-Ring.

Architectural twin to the Kunsthistorisches Museum opposite, the Natural History Museum contains exhibits ranging from insects to dinosaurs, and a highly regarded collection of meteorites. The vast reserves derive in part from the private collections of François de Lorraine (1708–1765), husband of Maria Theresa. The Children's Room (Kindersaal) is a great family attraction. Some of the highlights include the 25,000-year-old figurine,*Venus of Willendorf*, a 117-kg (260-pound) giant topaz, and Maria Theresa's exquisite jewel bouquet made of precious stones.

Museums of the Belvedere

Both open Tues–Sun 10am–5pm. Oberes (Upper) Belvedere; Prinz-Eugen-Strasse 27, Tram D. Unteres (Lower) Belvedere, Rennweg 6a, Tram 71.

The Kunsthistorisches Museum achieves its balanced presentation of European art because Austrian art is housed separately in the twin palaces of the Belvedere.

You'll find the Museum Mittelalterlicher Österreichischer Kunst (Museum of Medieval Austrian Art) in the Orangerie, the Österreichisches Barockmuseum (Museum of Austrian Baroque) in the Lower Belvedere, and Österreichische Galerie des 19. und 20. Jahrhunderts (Austrian Gallery of the 19th and 20th Centuries) in the Upper Belvedere.

The **Museum of Austrian Baroque Art** presents the colorful epitome of 18th-century Vienna with warm portraits of Maria

Theresa and her husband François de Lorraine. It includes paintings by Gran, Maulbertsch, and Rottmayr, and sculpture by

Donner and Permoser, most notably the latter's *Apotheosis* of Prince Eugene in the Hall of Mirrors. Commissioned by the prince himself, it shows Eugene as Hercules spurning Envy and trying to silence Fame's trumpet.

> **Viennese German is peppered with Yiddish:** *Mischpoche* (family), *nebbich* (so what!), *Haberer* (boy-friend), *meschugge* (crazy).

The **Museum of Medieval Austrian Art** (access through the Museum of Austrian Baroque) has fine examples of 15th-century statuary and altarpieces from the Tyrol, Salzburg, Lower Austria, and Styria.

The **Austrian Gallery of the 19th and 20th Centuries** in the upper palace reflects the Austro-Hungarian empire's image as a declining world power, culminating in a grand last artistic fling around 1900.

After extensive renovation in the 1990s, a new restaurant and bookshop have been installed. The ground floor is also devoted to temporary exhibitions and a permanent collection of post-1918 Austrian art.

It is best to start on the first floor, devoted principally to the magnificent collection of paintings created around 1900. Look for Gustav Klimt's *The Kiss* and a splendid study of the city's great bourgeoisie in his portrait of *Frau Bloch.* Vienna's new proletariat found its painter in Egon Schiele, especially in his anguished and poignant *The Family, The Artist's Wife,* and *Death and the Maiden.* Also on display are the early Expressionist works of Oskar Kokoschka, his lyrical but profoundly psychological portraits such as *Carl Moll* and the *Portrait of Mother,* and his *Still Life with Ram and Hyacinth.*

Also on the first floor is a small but impressive collection of Impressionist and Post-Impressionist art with paintings by

Monet, Renoir, Cézanne, Van Gogh, and Edvard Munch, and sculptures by Rodin, Degas, and Renoir.

The more formal styles that preceded Austria's revolutionary trio and the Impressionists are represented on the second floor. Three rooms show the Neo-Classical world of the late 18th and early 19th century with works by Swiss-born Angelika Kauffmann, German Romantics Caspar David Friedrich and Carl Blechen. These dissolve into the plain and simple Biedermeier life, Vienna's "*Backhendlzeit*" (Roast Chicken Era) typified by Josef Danhauser and Ferdinand Waldmüller.

Graphische Sammlung Albertina

Temporarily Makartgasse 3, open 10am–5pm, closed Monday, U-Bahn 1,2, 4: Karlsplatz.
One of the world's finest collections of graphic art is housed in the Albertina (undergoing extensive renovation

---

Prince Eugene of Savoy (1663–1736)

Skeptical by nature, the Viennese have few authentic heroes — and, ironically, the greatest was a Frenchman who become the supreme Austrian patriot. A unique blend of military courage, culture, and human warmth, Prince Eugene of Savoy was born in Paris in 1663. Unsuccessful in establishing a military career in his own county, the prince spent a period in a monastery and then went to Austria to seek his fortune.

Denied a military career in Louis XIV's Versailles, he arrived in Vienna in 1683, just in time to help out with the campaigns against the Turks. Over the next 30 years he fought brilliantly for Austria against the Turks, and the French, rising to the position of commander-in-chief in 1697. Small of stature and always dressed in a rough brown uniform, simple as a monk's, he was known to his soldiers as "the little Capuchin."

at the south end of the Hofburg at Albertinaplatz 1). Named after Maria Theresa's son-in-law, Duke Albert of Saxony-Teschen, it was founded in 1781 and now holds over 40,000 original drawings and more than one million wood and copper-plate prints.

The collection represents virtually every major artist from the 15th century to the present, including priceless works by Dürer, da Vinci, Michelangelo, Raphael, Titian, Rembrandt, Rubens, Van Gogh, Toulouse-Lautrec, Beardsley, and Grosz.

> **Condescending but only mildly disparaging, Austrians like to refer to Germans as *Piefke*.**

Facsimiles of the best-known masterpieces are on permanent display, while original drawings are exhibited in special shows, changing some six times a year, each devoted to a particular period, style, or theme. Any of the drawings may be seen on written request.

Other Museums

Museum Modernen Kunst Stiftung Ludwig (Ludwig Foundation's Modern Art Museum). *Open 10am–6pm, closed Monday; Palais Liechtenstein, Fürstengasse 1, Tram D: Bauernfeldplatz.* The impressive selection of 20th-century art includes paintings by Kandinsky, Kokoschka, Jawlensky, Klee, Ernst, Magritte, and Warhol.

Akademie der Bildenden Künste (Academy of Fine Arts). *Open Tues–Sun 10am–4pm, Sat guided tour 10:30am, Schillerplatz 3, U-Bahn 1, 2, 4: Karlsplatz.* Few art academies can rival its outstanding collection of European painting from the 14th century to the present day. Its highlights include *The Last Judgment* by Hieronymus Bosch, works by Rubens, Rembrandt, Van Dyck, Pieter de Hooch and Tiepolo.

Jüdisches Museum (Jewish Museum). *Open 10am–6pm, Thurs to 8pm, closed Saturday, Dorotheergasse 11, U-Bahn*

1, 3: Stephansplatz. This recent addition to the Vienna museum scene (1993) is housed in the 18th-century Palais Eskeles, formerly the property of a prominent Jewish financier. With modern audio-visual techniques, it traces the history of the city's Jewish community from the Middle Ages, through the years of its illustrious contributions to Viennese culture, to its extermination by German and Austrian Nazis in World War II. Temporary exhibitions are also staged here, usually devoted to prominent artists, writers and other historical figures of

The gold and jewels at the Schatzkammer Museum really have razzle-dazzle.

Viennese life. Despite the community's tragic end, the museum's atmosphere is positive, reinforced by a cheerful café and bookstore on the ground floor.

Hofburg Museums. *Michaelerplatz 1; open 10am–4pm, closed Tues. Tram 1, 2 D or J: Burgring; U-Bahn 2: Babenbergerstrasse or Herrengasse.* The palace's museums exhibit most of the vast personal fortune of the Habsburgs. The **Schatzkammer** (treasury), in the Schweizerhof (The Swiss Court), contains a dazzling display of the insignia of the old Holy Roman Empire. Highlights are the Imperial Crown of pure unalloyed gold set with pearls and unpolished emeralds, sapphires, and rubies. First used in the year A.D. 962 for the coronation of Otto the Great in Rome, it moved on to Aachen and Frankfurt for crowning successors. Also on display are the sword of Charlemagne and the Holy Lance, which dates back to the Merovingian kings and is said to have pierced the body of Christ on the Cross. Other intriguing artifacts include a unicorn's horn; a "viper tongue credenza" used to render poisoned food edible; and an agate bowl, reputed to be the Holy Grail used by Christ at the Last Supper.

To the right of the Hofburg rotunda coming from the Michaelerplatz is the **Hofsilber und Tafelkammer** (Court Silver Depot and Tableware Collection). On display here are the priceless Chinese, Japanese, French Sèvres, and German Meissen services amassed by the Habsburgs over six centuries of weddings and birthdays. Highlights are a 140-piece service in vermeil and a Neo-Renaissance centerpiece given to Emperor Franz Joseph by Queen Victoria in 1851.

Perhaps the most Viennese collection in the Hofburg is the exquisite **Sammlung alter Musikinstrumente** (Musical Instruments Collection), in the Neue Burg's National Library. There you'll find 360 pieces of great historical interest, in particular the Renaissance instruments which represent practically everything played

Keyboard instruments have been crucial to the Viennese musical tradition.

up to the 17th century. Also on view are Haydn's harpsichord, Beethoven's piano of 1803, and an 1839 piano used by Schumann and Brahms.

More mundane but quite touching is the Wiener **Strassenbahnmuseum** (Vienna Tram Museum). *Open early May to early October, Fri, Sat, Sun 9am–4pm, Erdbergstrasse 109, U-Bahn 3, tram 18,72: Schlachthausgasse.* Housed in the Erdberg depot, the museum high-lights the development of public trans-

> The Viennese do not consider it morbid to be interested in funerals and admire *eine schöne Leich'* (a fine corpse).

port, from horse-drawn tram to modern streetcar. The museum also organizes city tours in an old-fashioned tram starting from Karlsplatz Fri, Sat, Sun at 9:30am, 11:30am, and 1:30pm.

Friedensreich Hundertwasser's eccentric **KunstHaus Wien** (see page 65), *open daily 10am–7pm, Untere Weissgerberstrasse 13 (wheelchair access) Tram N, O: Radetzkyplatz,* is devoted to the 20th-century artist's own col-orful works and temporary shows of his contemporaries.

Museumsquartier. *Museumsplatz U-Bahn 2,3: Volksthe-ater.* This sprawling modern museum complex is currently being built in the former Fischer von Erlach's 18th-century Hofstallungen (imperial stables). At present, it houses in temporary quarters the **Architekturzentrum,** (Museum of Modern Architecture) and Zoom-Kindermuseum, a **chil-dren's museum,** devoted to interactive games and educa-tional activities, but mostly for German-speaking children. When completed (projected date: 2002), the complex will embrace a series of modern art museums, artists' studios, and other multi-media installations. (A tobacco museum sponsored by a local manufacturer is also on the premises.)

Many of the city's most fascinating museums are devoted to its great men (so far no women).

Sigmund Freud Museum. *Open July–Sept 9am–6pm, Oct–June 9am–4pm; Berggasse 19, Tram D: Schlickgasse.* Devoted to the father of psychoanalysis, the best arranged of these "personal" museums makes up for the hostility with which most Viennese received him during his lifetime. His Vienna home has become a mecca for practitioners, students, and patients of psychoanalysis from all over the world. Freud lived here from 1891 until the arrival of the Nazis in 1938. A photograph in the museum shows the house draped with a swastika. All has been faithfully reconstituted by his disciples with original furniture and belongings, including his old hats, his walking stick, and suitcases initialed S.F. (The original sofa has stayed in the house of his London exile.)

Except for Mozart's, all the composers' museums have the same opening hours: *9am–12:15pm, 1pm–4:30pm, closed Monday.*

Schubert Museum. *Nussdorferstrasse 54, Tram 37,38: Canisiusgasse.* This is the house, now meticulously restored, where the composer was born on 31 January 1797.

Haydn Museum. *Haydngasse 19, U-Bahn 3: Zieglergasse.* This is where the composer lived from 1797 till his death on 31 May 1809. His two oratorios *The Creation* and *The Seasons* were conceived and written in this house.

Beethoven Museum. *Probusgasse 6, Tram 37: Geweygasse.* This is the Heiligenstadt house where the great composer wrote his fourth, fifth, and seventh symphonies. It was here that he also composed his famous and tragic *Heiligenstadt Testament* in which he told his two brothers of his encroaching deafness.

Mozart Museum. This museum is located in the Figarohaus (see page 29), *open 9am–6pm, closed Monday, Domgasse 5, U-Bahn 1, 3: Stephansplatz.*

THE OTHER VIENNA

Beyond the Innere Stadt and outside the imperial world of the Hofburg and Schönbrunn lies the heart of everyday Vienna. Take a stroll up Mariahilferstrasse, the city's most popular shopping street, or visit Café Sperl, on Gumpendorfer Strasse. Running along the Linke Wienzeile are the fruit, vegetable, and meat stalls of the Naschmarkt. Notice the Jugendstil façade of Majolikahaus at number 40, designed by Otto Wagner.

Equally colorful is the whimsical **Hundertwasserhaus,** a hugely popular tourist attraction dismissed by architectural purists as a bit of a joke. This public housing complex in Kegelgasse was designed by Austria's best-known, if not most admired, living artist, Friedensreich Hundertwasser. The undulating façades of 52 apartments are decorated with bright paintwork, tiles, ceramics, and onion domes. In the nearby Weissgerberstrasse is Hundertwasser's own museum, the Kunsthaus Wien (see page 63).

One "excursion" that is popular with the Viennese may surprise some foreign visitors: the **Zentralfriedhof** (Central Cemetery), Simmeringer Hauptstrasse 234, tram 71, 72. Handsome or kitschy funerary monuments

The façades of some of Vienna's private homes are a bit wackier than others.

pay homage here to the city's great: Beethoven, Schubert, Brahms, Arnold Schönberg, and writers Arthur Schnitzel and Franz Werfel. Look for the cenotaph to Mozart, buried elsewhere in an unmarked pauper's grave A detailed map of the cemetery is available at Tor (Gate) 2.

Prater Park

Over the Aspernbrücke, cross the Danube canal at the junction of Franz-Josefs-Kai and Stubenring. This takes you to **Prater** park, an old-fashioned amusement park featuring roller coasters, discos, shooting ranges, restaurants, and beer halls. In the good old days, the Prater cafés were serenaded by the ubiquitous Strauss family and their archrival, Joseph Lanner.

If the Stephansdom had not already become the undisputed symbol of the city, the Prater's **Riesenrad** (giant Ferris wheel) would certainly have laid claim — especially after the famous ride of Orson Welles and Joseph Cotten in Carol Reed's film *The*

Third Man. Built in 1897, by English engineer Walter B. Basset, it is one of the oldest and largest Ferris wheels in the world, 65 m (213 ft) high, and provides a great view over the city and the surrounding countryside. (The original wheel was built just five years earlier by American engineer George Ferris for the Columbian Fair in Chicago in 1893.)

Round and round she goes — the Reisenrad at Prater Park is a Vienna favorite.

Next to the Riesenrad is the terminal of the Lilliputbahn (**Lilliputian Railroad**), which on summer weekends provides transport to the Fair Trade Grounds, the Planetarium, and the Prater Museum.

Donauinsel

You can reach the real Danube River (as opposed to the Danube Canal) along Lassallestrasse and over the Reichsbrücke. A man-made recreation island featuring beaches, barbecue picnic areas, and sports facilities, the **Donauinsel** runs 21 km (13 miles) down the middle of the river.

You may be disappointed to discover that the "Blue Danube" is actually yellowish brown in color. This is due to the lime content of the riverbed. Be patient and continue on the Wagramerstrasse, past the attractive modern complex of buildings forming the **UNO-City** (officially Vienna International Center, guided tours Mon–Fri 11am and 2pm) to the **Alte**

> For the price of a coffee, you can stay in a coffeehouse all day and read all the international newspapers you like.

Donau (the Old Danube). This self-contained arm of the river is closed off for sailing, fishing, and bathing and is as blue as blue can be, especially on a sunny day. In the heart of the working-class 21st and 22nd districts, the banks are lined with beaches, marinas, and neat little gardens.

The **Donaupark** links the old and new Danube. More tranquil than the Prater, it has been laid out with beautiful flower beds, an artificial lake, and sports arenas. It also features a chair lift and the 252-m- (872-ft-) tall **Donauturm** (Danube Tower), with fine views from its terrace and revolving restaurant. From here you can see across the city to the Wienerwald and the Abbey of Klosterneuburg and beyond.

Vienna's Suburbs

You should devote at least one full day to the 19th District of
Döbling, without a doubt the most gracious and elegant of
Vienna's suburbs. Stretching from the Danube Canal to the
slopes of the Wienerwald, Döbling includes Sievering,
Grinzing, Heiligenstadt, Nussdorf, and Kahlenberg. It is dotted with villas, parks, vineyards, and, of course, the Heuriger
wine gardens, which are especially popular in **Grinzing.**

If you do not have a car, start your tour by catching Tram
37 in front of the Votivkirche at Schottentor, and take it to
Heiligenstadt, the heart of Vienna's "Beethoven country."
You may want to stop off en route in Döbling at the **Villa
Wertheimstein** (Döblinger Hauptstrasse 96), a masterpiece
of 19th-century Biedermeier architecture, full of period
pieces, and featuring a lovely English garden. At the end of
the line (Heiligenstädter Park), walk across the park past the
monument to Beethoven to Pfarrplatz 2, the prettiest of the
composer's many Viennese homes.

Heiligenstadt and the other neighborhoods of Döbling
provide a vital clue to the secret of Vienna's charm. Vienna
is not a conventional big city, but rather a collection of villages clustered around the Innere Stadt. These village-sub-
urbs provide a convenient getaway from what the Viennese
call the *Hektik* of metropolitan life.

For a pleasant outing in the country, drive your car (or take
the 38S bus from Grinzinger Allee) up to the Höhenstrasse
leading to Kahlenberg and Leopoldsberg on the northern
slopes of the Wienerwald. The route offers a grandiose view
of the city and surrounding country. You'll find it difficult to
believe that you're still inside the city limits. If time permits,
get out and walk around — the road has several inns and
cafés where you can stop for a drink or a bite to eat.

Beethoven locked himself in here at Heiligenstadt, where some of his most notable works were penned.

Since the end of the 18th century, the heights of **Kahlenberg** have been dotted with fashionable summer homes offering what is known as *Sommerfrische* (cool summer respite from the city heat). During two steaming hot days in July 1809, the Viennese aristocracy had a grandstand view of Napoléon's Battle of Wagram against the Austrians. Sipping cool Nussdorfer white wine, they watched the maneuvering of 300,000 soldiers on the far side of the Danube and the slaughter of approximately 40,000 Austrians and 34,000 Frenchmen.

The Höhenstrasse goes as far as **Leopoldsberg,** the very edge of the Wienerwald and the extreme eastern point of the European Alps. On a clear day, you can see about 100 km (62 miles) eastwards from the terrace of the **Leopoldskirche** to the Carpathian mountains of Slovakia.

A short detour to the north (about 7 km/4 miles) takes you to the imposing Augustine abbey of **Klosterneuburg.** A fanciful story claims it was founded by Duke Leopold III of Babenberg in 1106 on the spot where his bride's lost veil was discovered by his hunting dogs. In fact its foundation is earlier, but little of the original edifice remains. Karl VI, who was

> *"Sissy" is only one of a whole string of still popular aristocratic nicknames — Puppi, Menni, Mitzi, Süssi.*

very much taken with Spain, undertook expansive (and expensive) alterations in the 18th century, making it a Baroque version of the Escorial. He wanted a combination palace and church with nine domes, each topped with a crown of the House of Habsburg. Only two were completed in his lifetime: the crown of the empire on the big dome and of the Austrian archduchy on the little one. Maria Theresa had neither the desire nor the money to carry on.

Klosterneuburg also boasts a brand new museum of modern art, the **Sammlung Essl** (Essl Collection), a private foundation devoted to avant-garde Austrian artists and their representative American and European contemporaries (*An der Donau-Au 1, Tel. 0800-232800, open Tues–Sat 10am–7pm, Wed to 9pm*).

The Baroque ornamentation is indeed impressive, but the whole trip is made worthwhile by the **Leopoldskapelle,** with its magnificent **Verdun Altar** of 1181 containing 45 enameled panels depicting scenes from the scriptures. It served as a *biblia pauperum* — graphic bible for the poor who could not read the stories.

DANUBE VALLEY

One of the great attractions of Vienna is the fact that it embraces an enchanting countryside and is within easy reach of many other fascinating historic sites. If, however, your visit gives you time for only one side-trip it should unquestionably be along the Danube Valley, in particular the magical area known as the Wachau between the historic towns of Melk and Krems.

Just an hour's drive west of Vienna, this is where the Danube Valley is at its most picturesque — by turns charming and smiling with vineyards, apricot orchards, and rustic villages, then suddenly forbidding with ruined medieval castles and rocky cliffs half hidden in mist.

You cannot wax too romantic in describing the scenery, for this is a landscape whose atmosphere is heavy with myth. Legend has it that the Burgundy kings of the medieval German epic, the *Nibelungenlied,* passed this spot en route to the kingdom of the Huns. The Crusaders also passed through here on their way to the Holy Land.

The Melk abbey was once a safe haven on the banks of the not-so-blue Danube.

Take the Danube River steamer if you simply want to sit and dream as this mythical world passes you by. For a closer look at the towns and castles on the way it's best to travel around car.

On a leisurely tour of the Danube Valley 84 km (52 miles) by the Westautobahn from Vienna, the Benedictine abbey of **Melk** (*Stift Melk*) makes an ideal starting point. Towering high above the river on a protruding rock, this is one of the region's most majestic sights. If it looks uncommonly like a fortress, it is because its strategic position overlooking a bend in the river made it a favored point of defense from the time of the

Romans. The Babenberg predecessors of the Habsburgs had a palace stronghold here in the 10th century, which they handed over to the Benedictines in 1106. The monks gradually turned the sanctified fortress into a fortified sanctuary of noble proportions, gracefully enhanced by the Baroque transformations of architect Jakob Prandtauer in 1702.

The abbey lies stretched along the trapezoid-shaped cliffs that line the river valley. Two towers, together with the octagonal dome and the lower Bibliothek (Library) and Marmorsaal (Marble Hall), form a harmonious group that softens the somewhat forbidding landscape. The interior of the church is rich in reds and golds with a high altar by Antonio Beduzzi and superbly sculpted pulpit, choir, and confessionals. The ceiling frescoes are by Johann Michael Rottmayr, whose work also adorns Vienna's Karlskirche.

Before crossing the river Danube, make a quick detour to the village of **Mauer,** 10 km (6 miles) due east of Melk to see the late-Gothic wooden altarpiece in the parish church. The work, by an anonymous local artist around 1515, depicts the *Adoration of the Virgin Mary* with a wealth of vivid detail.

The faithful return better armed to the paganism of the crumbling castles on the Danube. The Wachauer Strasse, along the north bank of the river, is dotted with apricot orchards and sunny vineyards, 18th-century Weinhüterhütten (vine-guard's huts), and villages teeming with Heuriger wine gardens.

On the opposite bank, you can see Schönbühel and the 13th-century ruins of **Burg Aggstein.** The castle was once owned by a robber baron named Jörg Scheck vom Wald, popularly known as "Schreckenwald" (Terror of the Forest). One of his favorite exercises was to lead prisoners to his rose garden, on the edge of a sheer precipice, where they were given the choice of either starving to death — few opted for eating the roses — or ending it quickly by jumping 53 m (175 ft) to the rocks below.

Back on the happier north bank, visit the town of Spitz, with its lovely late-Gothic **St. Mauritius church.** It's known for its statues of the apostles in the 1380 organ gallery, and the Baroque painting of the *Martyrdom of St. Mauritius* by Kremser (Martin Johann) Schmidt. In the village of St. Michael, look for seven stone hares perched on the roof of the 16th-century church. These commemorate a particularly vicious winter when snowdrifts were said to have enabled the animals to jump clear over the church. In the village of Weissenkirchen is a fortified church (religion and war always went hand in hand in this region) which was originally surrounded by four towers, a moat, ramparts, and 44 cannons to fend off the Turks.

> Austrians love diminutives: *Beisl* (bistro) means "little house" from the Hebrew *Beth,* while *Häusl,* also "little house," is a toilet.

The most romantic of these medieval towns is **Dürnstein,** famous as the site of Richard the Lion-Heart's imprisonment in 1192–1193. Devastated by the Swedish army in 1645, the castle of Kuenringer is more interesting to look at from below than it is to visit. But do make a point of seeing Dürnstein's **abbey church,** a Baroque structure with a splendid carved wooden door to the abbey courtyard and an imposing statue of the resurrected Christ at the church entry.

Your journey along the Wachauer will end delightfully with a visit to **Krems,** heart of the region's wine industry and historically one of the Danube Valley's most important trade centers. Today, you can enjoy its superb Gothic, Renaissance, and Baroque residences on tranquil, tree-shaded squares — unspoiled by early 19th-century Biedermeier construction.

Park on the Südtiroler Platz and walk through the 15th-century Steiner Tor (town gate) with its Gothic pepper pot towers. Turn immediately left up the Schmidgasse to the Körnermarkt and the Dominikanerkirche (Dominican Church), transformed into an important museum of medieval art. Continue round to the Pfarrplatz, dominated by the **Pfarrkirche,** a lovely church redone (1616–1630) by two Italian architects and decorated with altar paintings by Franz Anton Maulbertsch and the masterful frescoes of Kremser Schmidt. The church epitomizes the town's own happy marriage of Italian and Austrian tastes.

The oldest square in Krems, the Hoher Markt, boasts a masterpiece of Gothic residential architecture, the arcaded **Gozzoburg,** built around 1270. Take a stroll along the Untere Landstrasse to see the elegant Baroque façades (numbers 41, 4, and 1) and the fine Renaissance **Rathaus** (town hall).

Vienna is graced with countless steeples and spires, jutting into the Austrian sky.

By now you will feel ready to avail yourself of the local "new wine" served in one of the leafy arcaded courtyards along the Obere Landstrasse (Krems's main thoroughfare). An outstanding example of 16th-century Italian Renaissance architecture along this pedestrianized shopping street is the Gasthof Alte Post (at number 32).

Let somebody else chauffeur you back to Vienna (90 km/56 miles on route S3).

WIENERWALD

If the idea of Vienna is incomplete without the Danube, there would still be something missing if you left out the Wienerwald (Vienna Woods) — and not just its northern slopes along the Höhenstrasse to Kahlenberg and Leopoldsberg. To properly appreciate the Wienerwald, you must visit the villages hidden away in the forest to the south and southwest of Vienna.

Take the Breitenfurterstrasse (behind Schönbrunn Palace) out to Perchtoldsdorf, a serene little village amid heather-covered hills, vineyards, and fir trees. Continue south to Burg Liechtenstein, a "ruined castle" built in 1873 on the site of the 12th-century home of the Liechtenstein dynasty. The park is an ideal spot for a picnic. In **Mödling** you can see the 15th-century Gothic Spitalkirche (church) and the house (Hauptstrasse 79) where Beethoven worked on his *Missa Solemnis*.

Turn west along route 11 to Hinterbrühl. Romantics like to believe that the picturesque old mill, Höldrichsmühle (converted into an inn), is where Franz Schubert wrote songs for the miller's daughter Rosi (*"Die schöne Müllerin"*) in 1823. Actually the whole story originated in an 1864 operetta devoted to the composer's life. But the inn's wines can make believers of us all.

The road takes you through gentle hills down to the Sattelbach Valley and the Cistercian abbey of **Heiligenkreuz** (Holy Cross), founded by the Babenberg family in 1133. Heiligenkreuz is named after the relic of a piece of the True Cross, given to Austria by the King of Jerusalem in the 12th century and now kept in the tabernacle behind the high altar. You reach the basilica via a courtyard, which features a **Trinity Column** (Pillar of the Plague), the work of Baroque artist Giovanni Giuliani, who also designed the basilica's splendid choir stalls. The structure has preserved the asymmetrical Romanesque western façade, and Giuliani's elegant work on the choir does not clash with the essential simplicity of the interior, a recognized triumph of spatial harmony in late-medieval architecture. Along the south side of the basilica is a graceful 13th-century cloister with 300 red columns.

In the town **churchyard** you'll find a tomb bearing the inscription: *"Wie eine Blume sprosst der Mensch auf und wird gebrochen"* ("Like a flower, the human being unfolds–and is broken"). This is the grave of Mary Vetsera, the 17-year-old young lady who died in 1889 at Mayerling in a murder-suicide with Crown Prince Rudolf, heir to the Austro-Hungarian Empire.

In the autumn of 1888, Rudolf, the only son of Franz Joseph and Elisabeth, fell in love with Mary, daughter of the Hungarian Countess Vetsera. But the Pope refused to annul the archduke's existing marriage. Frustrated with the conservative politics of his father, Franz Joseph, and miserable with his hopeless love affair, Rudolf decided on 29 January 1889 to spirit Mary away to his hunting lodge in **Mayerling** (4 km/ $2^{1}/_{2}$ miles southwest of Heiligenkreuz).

In the middle of the night Rudolf shot Mary with a revolver, covered her body with flowers, and sat beside her till dawn, when he shot himself through the right temple, using a mirror so as not to miss. The scandalous event has been so enshrined in cheap romantic history and Hollywood hokum that it comes almost as a shock to see the actual signpost outside Heiligenkreuz pointing to Mayerling, 3 km (2 miles) to the west. To hush the scandal-mongers, the hunting lodge where the tragedy occurred was demolished shortly thereafter, on the orders of Franz Joseph, and replaced with a Carmelite convent whose nuns keep a vow of lifelong silence.

From Mayerling, drive on through the wildly romantic Helenental Valley to the spa of **Baden,** 25 km (16 miles) south of Vienna. Enjoyed by the Romans and made fashionable by Franz I in 1803, Baden became the very symbol of upright Viennese Biedermeier prosperity. Occasionally bathing in the

Winemaking is an Austrian tradition — a visit is not complete without sampling some of the many varietals.

36°C (97°F) sulphurous waters to deal with a spot of rheumatism, the gentry of Vienna built their summer villas here and wandered in the spa's Kurpark to the strains of Johann Strauss's waltzes. On a higher musical plane, Beethoven had completed here the *Ode to Joy* for his 9th Symphony.

The king of Biedermeier architecture was Josef Kornhäusel, and his Neo-Classical façades set the tone for the town's cozy conformity. The best example of his work is the Ionic-porticoed Greek temple Rathaus, with Joseph Klieber's allegorical statues celebrating the ideals of the age: *Gerechtigkeit* (justice) and *Klugheit* (wisdom).

Note that Baden's wonderfully therapeutic thermal waters can still be enjoyed in the indoor thermal pool (Brusattiplatz 4); the open-air thermal pools (Helenen Strasse 19–21); and the mineral water thermal pools (Marchetti Strasse 13).

Drive home via **Gumpoldskirchen,** a picturesque wine village with a lovely Gothic church, 16th-century town hall, and first-rate Heuriger wine gardens.

TO THE EAST

The Bratislava road east from Vienna (No. 9) follows the Danube and traces the ancient Eastern European boundary of the Roman empire. Just 36 km (22 miles) along, you come to the remains of **Carnuntum.** Once the capital of the Roman province of Pannonia (embracing much of modern Hungary and eastern Austria), it has now been absorbed by the town of Petronell. In the second century, under Hadrian and Marcus Aurelius, Carnuntum was a thriving commercial center. Here Celtic timber merchants and gold-, silver-, and coppersmiths lived in prosperous harmony with 6,000 Roman soldiers guarding the imperial outpost against barbarian invasion.

Stop on the right before you reach the town and walk to the amphitheater, where spectators used to watch gladiators slaughter wild animals — and each other. Today it is the site of a summer festival.

From Petronell drive 5 km (3 miles) south to **Rohrau,** the birthplace of Joseph Haydn. You can visit his beau-

The entrance to the Kunst Forum was designed in the Jugendstil style.

tifully restored thatched-roof farmhouse where he was born in 1732. Concerts are held regularly here during the spring and summer. Nearby is the Schloss Rohrau, the Baroque castle of the Harrach family, who were early patrons of young Haydn. The castle has a fine collection of 17th-century Spanish, Flemish, and Italian art.

Continue on to one of Austria's most delightful lakes, the **Neusiedler See.** This birdwatchers' paradise teems with heron, teal, waterfowl, wild geese, and egret. The water is so shallow that it's possible to wade right across — only a few spots are more than 1.5 m (5 ft) deep. If you do cross the lake make sure you're armed with your passport and a visa for your arrival on the other side — the southern end of the lake belongs to Hungary. Flat-bottomed boats can be hired for fishing. In winter you can go skating and ice-sailing; in summer operettas are performed on the landing stages.

> **Nothing politically correct about Viennese admiration for titles: Whatever her qualifications, the wife of a professor becomes** *Frau Professorin.*

Along the lake's western shores are the villages of **Rust** and **Mörbisch.** Both are famous for the storks that favor their chimneys for nesting. Rust has nearly 50 stork nests on its rooftops. In Mörbisch, right on the Hungarian border, walk along the unspoiled shady lanes with their spotless whitewashed houses colorfully decorated with beautiful flowers and bouquets of maize. The wine gardens here are truly idyllic.

On the way back to Vienna, pass through the Baroque town of **Eisenstadt,** 52 km (32 miles) southwest of Vienna, where Joseph Haydn lived and worked for many years as musical director for Hungarian prince, Paul Anton Esterhazy. The composer is buried here.

Vienna Highlights

Belvedere. Magnificent Baroque residence of Prince Eugene of Savoy, two palaces overlooking formal gardens. Fine collection of 20th-century art (Österreichische Galerie: Klimt, Schiele, Kokoschka) in Oberes (Upper) Belvedere; Prinz-Eugen-Strasse 27, Tram D. Baroque art in Unteres (Lower) Belvedere, Rennweg 6a, Tram 71. Both open Tues–Sun, 10am–5pm, gardens open daily sunrise to sunset.

Graben. City's most elegant shopping area, including adjacent Kohlmarkt's boutiques and Demel pastry shop. U-Bahn 1, 3: Stephansplatz.

Heuriger Wine Gardens. Romantic gardens in the leafy 19th district of Döbling. Come to sample new white wines and hear sentimental Viennese music. Most open daily afternoon till midnight. Trams 38, D, Bus 35A.

Hofburg (Imperial Palace). In Habsburgs' grandiose castle, see their Imperial Apartments, furniture and family jewels, museums of royal collections. (Wheelchair access.) Michaelerplatz 1; open 10am–6pm (museums till 4pm), closed Tues. Tram 1, 2 D or J: Burgring; U-Bahn 2: Babenbergerstrasse or Herrengasse.

Karlskirche. City's most important Baroque church, grandiose 18th-century copper-domed monument built to rival St Peter's, Rome. Daily 8am–7pm, Sunday 9am–7pm. U-Bahn 4: Karlsplatz.

Kunsthistorisches Museum (Fine Arts Museum). One of world's greatest collections of European art — Brueghel, Rembrandt, Vermeer, Titian, Giorgione, Caravaggio, Velázquez. (Wheelchair access.) Maria-Theresien-Platz. Closed Monday. Open 10am–6pm, Thursday to 9pm. U-Bahn 2: Babenbergerstrasse, Tram D, J, 1, 2: Burgring.

Prater Park. Huge park with popular amusements, including rollercoasters, shooting ranges, and beer halls. Particularly famous for *Riesenrad* giant Ferris wheel. *Volksprater* (amusement-park) open daily May–September, Christmas and New Year's holidays, 8am–11pm; mid-February–April, and October–mid-November, 10am–10pm; closed mid November–mid-February. U-Bahn 1 or tram O, 5, 21: Praterstern.

Schönbrunn. Maria Theresa's favorite palace, but also beloved by Franz Joseph and Elizabeth. Lovely park, fountains, and woods (wheelchair access). Schönbrunner Schlossstrasse 47; open daily April–October, 8:30am–5pm; November–March, to 4:30pm; park daily to sunset. U-Bahn 4 or tram 10, 48: Schönbrunn.

Spanish Riding School. Performances of the superb white Lipizzaner horses in the Hofburg's Winterreitschule (winter riding school). Josefsplatz; April–June, (closed July, August), then September–October, at 10:45am and 7pm, lasting 80 minutes; morning training (60 minutes) 10am and noon. U-Bahn 1,3: Stephansplatz.

Staatsoper (State Opera). One of the world's most famous opera houses. Season from 1 September to 30 June. Guided tours by appointment, Tel. 514 44 2613. (Wheelchair access.) Opernring 2; U-Bahn 4: Karlsplatz/Oper, Tram 1, 2 D or J: Oper.

Stephansdom (St. Stephan's Cathedral). The great Gothic and Romanesque cathedral is the perhaps the city's most beloved landmark. Great view from towers. North Tower (elevator) daily April–June and September–October 9am–6pm, July–August to 6:30pm, November–March, 8:30am–5pm. South Tower (343 steps) daily 9am–5:30pm, U-Bahn 1, 3: Stephansplatz.

WHAT TO DO

ENTERTAINMENT

Opera

There are people who wouldn't touch opera with the end of a barge pole — until they come to Vienna. Suddenly, in an atmosphere of sheer love, enthusiasm, and excitement that only the Viennese can muster, the most hardened resistance to this most challenging of musical forms just melts away. It's difficult to think of a cultural institution in another European capital that holds the privileged place of the **Staatsoper** (State Opera) in Vienna. Since this is Austria, try to make Mozart your first opera; after that you'll be ready to take on Wagner and even Alban Berg.

If you have tickets for a première or other gala performance, you should wear evening dress, though even on an ordinary night, people turn up in black tie or long dress.

There's also first-rate opera to be heard at the **Volksoper** (Währingerstraße 78), and operetta and ballet at the **Theater an der Wien** (Linke Wienzeile 6).

Music

In the two principal concert halls, the **Musikverein** (Dumbastraße 3) and the **Konzerthaus** (Lothringestraße 20), you can hear the Vienna Philharmonic and Vienna Symphony orchestras, and countless solo and chamber music recitals. You should also try to hear the celebrated **Wiener Sängerknaben** (Vienna Boys' Choir), who sing at Sunday Mass and other festivities in the Burgkapelle in the Hofburg.

Music in Vienna is not only fueled by its hallowed classical tradition, but also by the joy of its waltzes — music made

Catching a Mozart opera at the regal Staatsoper (State Opera House) is both a privilege and a pleasure.

famous around the world by Johann Strauss and his family. It can still be heard at concerts in the Stadtpark, in the Prater cafés, and in the Wienerwald Heurigen. Or make for the *Johann Strauss* riverboat moored on the Danube Canal to listen and dance to Strauss and Lanner. The more formal version can be enjoyed at the grand winter-season balls — organized by associations of doctors, lawyers, engineers, even *Fiaker* cab-drivers — the highlights being the Kaiserball (Emperor's Ball, without the emperor) on New Year's Eve in the Hofburg and the more republican Opernball (Opera Ball) in *Fasching* (carnival) season at the Staatsoper (see *Calendar of Events* page 90).

The music season runs from September to June, climaxing with the **Vienna Festival** (end of May to end of June). In July and August there are excellent summer concerts in the courtyard of the Rathaus, at Schönbrunn, and at Belvedere palace.

Theater

The **Burgtheater** (National Theater) is not just Vienna's proudest theater but also one of the leading ensembles of the German-speaking world. The **Akademietheater** focuses on modern and avant-garde drama. Performances are held all year round at Vienna's English Theater at Josefsgasse 12.

Nightlife

In recent years, the younger generations have breathed new life into Vienna's previously humdrum night scene. The city now numbers over 6,000 bars, nightclubs, discos, and cabarets — with many of the most popular bars staying open round the clock. North of Stephansdom, the happy-go-lucky

Be sure to get tickets far in advance for a performance at the Burgtheater — they are always in demand.

bars around Ruprechtsplatz, Seitenstettengasse, and Rabensteig form what is now popularly known as the **Bermudadreieck** (Bermuda Triangle) where people go to drop out of sight of more conventional establishments. Names change with each new owner but the bars stay full. More chic is the neighborhood around **Bäckerstrasse,** with the long-established bar and restaurant, Oswald & Kalb, at its center. The nightclubs around **Kärntnerstraße** cater to an expensive tourist trade. People with more traditional tastes enjoy the sentimental violin and zither music of the Balkan restaurants, the Schrammelmusik (violin, guitar and accordion trios) of the Heuriger wine gardens (see page 94), and the oom-pah-pah brass of the Prater.

SPORTS

With a foresight that nobody gives them credit for, the Habsburgs provided modern **joggers** with the perfect route, which doesn't require them to even leave the Innere Stadt. Start at the Burgtheater end of the Volksgarten near the monument to Empress Elisabeth, trot past the Theseus Temple, once around the duck pond to the statue of dramatist Franz Grillparzer, and then across Heldenplatz past Archduke Karl and Prince Eugene. Skirt the edge of the Neue Hofburg and whip around the Burggarten to salute the monuments to Goethe and Mozart. The entire route from Sissi to Wolfgang Amadeus and back should take even the most easy-going jogger less than 30 minutes.

Cycling and **in-line skating** are enjoyable ways of getting around Vienna — and of escaping traffic snarls. Bicycles can be rented inexpensively from any one of 160 Austrian railway stations. In Vienna, the three stations that rent bicycles are Westbahnhof, Wien Nord, and Floridsdorf. You can return your rented bicycle to any participating Austrian railway station. (You

Flea market finds and fruits are plentiful at the Naschmarkt — you're bound to find some surprises.

will need some form of ID card.) The free *See Vienna by Bike* brochure from the tourist information office lists bicycle rental firms, and also provides regional maps of cycling routes. The Prater has an in-line skate rental outlet near the Riesenrad Ferris wheel (Tel. 597 8288).

See Vienna's spectacular hinterland by **hiking** along the well-marked paths of the Wienerwald. In the winter, these same paths can be used for **cross-country skiing.**

The 21-km (13-mile) beach of the Donauinsel (see page 67) provides outdoor **swimming,** along with facilities for **waterskiing** and **windsurfing.** Döbling's Krapfenwaldlbad is a fashionable outdoor swimming pool, complete with champagne bar. Most handsome of indoor swimming pools is the Amalienbad, Reumannplatz 23, in Jugendstil décor with old-fashioned steambath and sauna.

Tennis and **squash** players will find dozens of courts in the Prater at Rustenschacher Allee and in the Donaupark,

Kratochwjlestraße, and Eiswerkstraße. There is a huge **bowling** alley in the Prater (Hauptallee 124). The Freudenau area of the Prater has an 18-hole **golf** course, **horse racing, horse riding,** and **polo.** You can also see professional football in the Prater, home of the town's first division team, Austria.

Ice-skating carries on year round in the Wiener Stadthalle, Vogelweidplatz 14.

SHOPPING

Not surprisingly the most important shopping attraction in Vienna, a town preoccupied by its history, is **antiques.** Furniture and *objets d'art* from all over the old empire have ended up here in the little shops in the Innere Stadt around the Josefsplatz: in Augustinerstrasse, Spiegelgasse, Plankengasse, and Dorotheergasse. You can still find authentic Rococo, Biedermeier, and Jugendstil pieces, including signed furniture of the great designers Michael Thonet and Josef Hoffmann.

Your best chance of finding a bargain is in the auction rooms of the **Dorotheum** (Dorotheergasse 17). This state pawnshop,

The Waltz

The waltz began as a heavy plodding triple-time German dance known as a *Ländler* which the Viennese transformed into a gay, whirling moment of fairyland. The man who brought the waltz to popular dance halls in 1819 was Joseph Lanner, leader of a small band. After he added a young viola player named Johann Strauss, the waltz took off in a big way. The group grew to an orchestra and Strauss broke away to form his own — Lanner sadly celebrating the occasion with his "Trennungswalzer" (Separation Waltz).

The two conducted a prolonged "Waltz War" for public favor in the cafés of the Prater. The rivalry ended amicably and Strauss played waltzes — adagio — at Lanner's funeral.

popularly known as "Tante Dorothee," was set up by Emperor Joseph I to enable the *nouveaux pauvres* to realize a quick return on heirlooms and possibly redeem them later during a more prosperous period. But it was also a kind of state-sponsored clearing house for stolen art objects, where the original owners could even buy their property back if the police had not managed to run down the thieves. Items are put on display before the sale, often in the windows of a bank opposite the auction rooms. If you feel uncertain about bidding, you can hire a licensed agent to do it for you for a small fee.

Still in the realm of the past are the great speciality shops for **coin-** and **stamp-collectors** (where else could you expect to find mint-condition Bosnia-Herzegovina issues of 1914?).

The national **Augarten porcelain** workshops still turn out hand-decorated Rococo chinaware, including figures of the Lipizzaner horses. **Petit-point embroidery** is available in the form of handbags, cushions, and other items with flower, folk, and opera motifs. Viennese craftsmen are also noted for their

ceramics, handmade dolls, enamel miniatures, and costume jewelry.

You will find the more elegant shops on the Kärntnerstrasse, Graben, and Kohlmarkt. Traditional Austrian costume (Trachten) has caught the whimsical attention of high fashion with the **Dirndl,** a pleated skirt with

No amusement park is ever really complete without a colorful carousel.

a blue- or pink-and-white apron tied at the waist and a white full-sleeved blouse under a laced bodice. For men the heavy woolen **Loden** cloth makes excellent winter coats.

The Saturday morning **flea market** on the Naschmarkt is a veritable Aladdin's Cave. It is situated next to the fruit and vegetable market at the Kettenbrückengasse underground station. The market caters mainly to youthful tastes, but you'll find there's something for everyone here. Each week a different provincial town brings in its bric-a-brac and miscellaneous treasures.

Children

Listed below are some suggestions for outings with the kids—which parents, too, might appreciate for a change of pace:

Prater amusement park features bowling alleys, riding stables, roller coasters, merry-go-rounds, and the biggest Ferris wheel in Europe.

Schönbrunn park has a zoo and an antique coach collection (Wagenburg).

Boating on the Alte Donau, where there are kayaks, rowing boats, and sailing boats for rent.

Ice-skating on the indoor rink in the Stadthalle, Vogelweidplatz, or, in the winter, on the outdoor rink at Lothringerstraße 22 near the Inter-Continental Hotel.

Swimming in public indoor or outdoor pools in all parts of Vienna, listed in the telephone book under "Badeanstalten" or "Städtische Bäder."

Dinosaurs and the Children's Room (Kindersaal) in the Naturhistorisches (Natural History) Museum.

Zoom-Kindermuseum (a children's museum) devoted to interactive games and educational activities in the new Museumsquartier.

Calendar of Events

(Detailed information on tickets, etc., available at Tourist Information Office, Tel. 2111 4222 or English-language website <http//info.wien.at> .)

January *Neujahrskonzert* (New Year's Day concert), 11am, Vienna Philharmonic's traditional recital in the Musikverein concert hall (see page 82); jazz-lovers' alternative: Vienna Art Orchestra, 9pm, Sofiensäle, Marxergasse 17; *Ball der Philharmoniker* (Philharmonic Ball) rivals Opera Ball for prestige, Musikverein.

February/March *Fasching* (Carnival) procession in Döbling; Opera Ball, *the* social event of the year at Staatsoper.

April *Ostermarkt* (Easter Market) country-fair atmosphere on Freyung in Innere Stadt; *Wiener Sängerknaben* (Vienna Boys' Choir) weekly Mass in Hofmusikkapelle; *OsterKlang Wien* (Vienna's Sounds of Easter) music festival.

May/June 1 May, traditional May Day celebrated at Prater amusement park; Vienna Marathon accompanied by popular festivities; *Wiener Festwochen* (Vienna Festival), music, dance, and theater at Theater an der Wien and Messepalast.

June *Regenbogen Parade* (Gay Rainbow Parade) on Ringstrasse; *Donaueninselfest* (Danube Island Festival) fun-fair festivities.

July/August *Jazzfest Wien* (Vienna Jazz Festival) at Staatsoper and Burgtheater; *Wiener Musiksommer*, summer festival of popular opera and operetta at Theater an der Wien.

September Schönbrunn Palace festival; In-line Skating Marathon on Ringstrasse.

October *Viennale* Film Festival.

November/December *Christkindlmarkt* (Christmas Market) carols, roast chestnuts, hot grog on Rathausplatz; New Year's Eve *Kaiserball* (Emperor's Ball) opens ball season in Hofburg; concerts, recitals throughout Innere Stadt.

EATING OUT

When it comes to Viennese cuisine, you must bear in mind that this city was once the center of the old Habsburg Empire of 60 million Eastern and Southern Europeans. The emperor and his archdukes and generals have gone, but not the Bohemian dumplings, the Hungarian goulash, the Polish stuffed cabbage, and Serbian *shashlik,* and the plum, cherry, and apricot brandies that accompany the Turkish coffee. And all are now frequently served with the lighter touch of the New Viennese Cuisine.

VIENNESE SPECIALITIES

Two Viennese staples that you're likely to come across immediately are the *Wiener Schnitzel* and the *Backhendl.* The *Wiener Schnitzel* is a large, thinly sliced cutlet of veal crisply sautéed in a coating of egg and seasoned breadcrumbs. *Backhendl* is roast chicken prepared in the same way. Viennese gourmets insist that the *Wiener Schnitzel* be served with cold potato or cucumber salad. You should also make sure that it is a cut of veal (*vom Kalb*) and not pork (*vom Schwein*), as in some of the cheaper estab-

There are a variety of marketplaces selling all sorts of Viennese goodies.

lishments. The *Backhendl* is sometimes served with *Geröstete* (sautéed potatoes).

Tafelspitz (boiled beef) was Emperor Franz Joseph's favorite dish, and to this day is a form of ambrosia to the Viennese. Spice it up with *Kren* (horseradish) and *Schnittlauchsauce* (chive sauce). Another culinary delight, originally from Hungary, is goulash — beef chunks stewed in onions, garlic, paprika, tomatoes, and celery. *Debreziner* sausages, *Köménymagleves Nokedival* (caraway-seed soup with dumplings), and apple soup (apples, cloves, cinnamon, white wine, lemon juice, sugar, and extra-thick cream) are three more Hungarian specialties.

From the Czech Republic comes delicious Prague ham and sauerkraut soup; from Polish Galicia, roast goose served with dumplings and red cabbage; and from Serbia, the peppery barbecued *cevapcici* meatballs and *schaschlik* brochettes of lamb with onions, and green and red peppers.

Dumplings *(Knödel)*, made from flour, yeast, or potatoes, are an Austrian staple served with the main course and in the soup. The *Marillenknödel* is a dessert dumpling, made of potato with a piping hot apricot inside. Another delicious dessert dumpling is the *Topfenknödel*, made with a cream-cheese filling.

Hot desserts are in fact a specialty and you should also try *Buchteln* or *Wuchteln*, yeast buns often filled with plum jam,

A Matter of Taste

A celebrated legal battle between Café Demel and Hotel Sacher resolved the contentious matter of who should have the right to the label "original Sachertorte" — the hotel won. But after delivering his verdict, on judicial grounds, the judge went off to eat his personal preference at Demel.

and from Hungary the *Palatschinken*, pancakes filled with jam or nuts. Finally, don't forget the *Apfelstrudel*, a flaky, almost transparent pastry filled with thinly sliced apples, raisins, and cinnamon.

Finally, there's the most famous and sinfully delicious chocolate cake in the world, the *Sachertorte*. Join in the endless debate over whether or not it should be split into two layers and where the apricot jam should go.

Wines and Wine Gardens

Wine in Vienna is almost always white wine, which the Viennese drink quite happily with meat and fish alike. The best known of Austrian white wines, the *Gumpoldskirchner*, has the full body and bouquet of its southern vineyards. The Viennese give equal favor to their own *Grinzinger, Nussdorfer, Sieveringer,* and *Neustifter*. From the Danube Valley, with an extra natural sparkle, come the *Kremser, Dürnsteiner* and *Langenloiser*.

Of the reds, the *Vöslauer*, produced in Bad Vöslau near Baden, and the *Kalterersee*, imported from South Tyrol (now Alto Adige

The cafés in Vienna range from bohemian to the most elegant atmospheres.

A street vendor flips his potato pancakes as some chestnuts roast nearby.

in Italy), are about the best. *Blaufränkisch* and *Zweigelt* are also reliable standbys.

To enjoy these wines in their original state, they should be ordered *herb* (dry). Often the producers will sweeten them for the foreign palate unless you specify otherwise. Perhaps the most pleasant thing about Viennese wine is the way in which it is drunk.

The Viennese have created a splendid institution, the **Heuriger,** where you can sip white wine on mild evenings under the stars. Winemakers are allowed by law to sell a certain amount of their new wine (also called *Heuriger*) directly to the public. They announce the new wine by hanging out a sprig of pine over the door and a sign saying *Ausg'steckt* (open). When the new wine has gone, the pine branch must be removed. The Heurigen of Grinzing are extremely popular, but many of the best ones are out in Nussdorf, Ober-Sievering, and Neustift. Heuriger gardens are generally open from mid-afternoon till late in the evening and on weekends for lunch. The season runs from March to October.

The local *Gösser* beer presents a fair challenge to the powerful *Pilsner Urquell* imported from the Czech Republic.

Among the brandies you should try the Hungarian *Barack* (apricot) and Serbian *Slivovitz* (plum).

Coffee and the Kaffeehaus

The varieties of coffee in Vienna are virtually endless, and there are names for every shade from black to white. Ask for *einen kleinen Mokka* and you'll get a small, strong black coffee and stamp yourself as someone of French or Italian taste. A *Kapuziner*, topped with generous dollops of cream, is already more Viennese; *ein Brauner*, with just a dash of milk, is as Viennese as can be. *Eine Melange* (pronounced "melanksch"), a mixture of milk and coffee, is designed for sensitive stomachs; *ein Einspänner*, with whipped cream in a tall glass, is for aunts on Sundays; *ein Türkischer*, prepared semi-sweet in a copper pot, is for addicts of the Balkan Connection.

The tradition of the Viennese *Kaffeehaus* dates back to the 17th century when, depending on which legend you choose, either a Polish spy named Kulczycki or a Greek merchant named Theodat opened the first café with a stock of coffee beans captured from the Turks. By the time of Maria Theresa the town was full of coffeehouses, fashionable and shady, where gentry and intellectuals mingled to pass the time of day. Some developed their own particular clientele — writers, artists, politicians, and the like — while the most prominent cafés (Griensteidl, Café Central, or Herrenhof) attracted all types.

After a post-war lull, the institution has made a grand comeback. In the Innere Stadt, the renovated Café Central and the more sedate Griensteidl are thriving once again. Café Hawelka, at Dorotheergasse 6, once popular with artists and antiques dealers, has become a hangout for the younger crowd. Artists now prefer Alt-Wien, at Bäckerstraße 9, and

Chocolate lovers beware — the Sachertorte could prove to be a dangerous treat.

the Kleines Café, Franziskanerplatz 3, with its superb interior design by architect Hermann Czech. Intellectuals have followed the example of the late Thomas Bernhard in favoring Café Bräunerhof, at Stallburggasse 2. This café is also popular with music-lovers for its weekend chamber-music recitals. Chess players with a killer instinct can be seen at the Café Museum, Friedrichstraße 6. Out in the Sixth District, Café Sperl, at Gumpendorfer Straße 11, is an elegant 100-year-old establishment with marble tables, Jugendstil chairs, an endless row of newspapers (including *The Times, Le Monde,* and *La Stampa*), and billiard tables for those who really can't bear to sit and do nothing.

Help with a Viennese Menu

Apfelstrudel	pastry filled with apples, raisins, and cinnamon
Auflauf	soufflé or casserole
Backhendl	chicken sautéed in egg and breadcrumbs
Bauernschmaus	meat served with dumplings and sauerkraut
Beuschel	chopped offal in sauce
Blunzn	black pudding
Buchteln/Wuchteln	yeast buns filled with plum jam

Debreziner	spicy Hungarian sausage
Eierschwammerl	mushrooms
Faschiertes	minced meat
Fleischlaberl	meat rissoles
Frittatensuppe	broth with sliced crêpes
Gefüllte Paprika	stuffed green pepper
Germknödel	yeast dumpling
Grießnockerlsuppe	semolina dumpling soup
Guglhupf	Viennese cake
Kaiserschmarrn	pancake served with fruit compote
Kalbsvögerl	knuckle of veal
Knödel	dumplings made from flour, potatoes, or yeast
Krenfleisch	boiled pork served with horseradish
Marillenknödel	apricot dumpling
Millirahmstrudel	strudel with sweet cheese filling
Nockerl	small dumpling
Palatschinken	pancakes filled with jam or nuts
Paradeiser	tomatoes
Powidl	plum sauce
Ribisel	red or black currants
Rostbraten	pot roast
Rotkraut	red cabbage
Sachertorte	chocolate cake
Schinkenfleckerl	baked noodles with chopped ham
Schwammerlsuppe	mushroom soup
Tafelspitz	boiled beef
Topfenknödel	dumpling with a cream-cheese filling
Topfenstrudel	strudel with cream cheese and raisins
Wiener Schnitzel	fillet of veal or pork fried in breadcrumbs
Zigeunerschnitzel	Wiener Schnitzel spiced with paprika
Zwetschkenröster	plum compote
Zwiebelrostbraten	beef steak served with fried onions

HANDY TRAVEL TIPS

An A–Z Summary of Practical Information

A

ACCOMMODATION (See also RECOMMENDED HOTELS, page 125)
The Vienna Tourist Board annually publishes a list of hotels, *Pensionen* (guest houses), and *Saison-Hotels* (student hostels used as hotels from July to September) with details about amenities, prices, and classifications. You can pick it up, along with an excellent free city map, from the Austrian Tourist Board in your country or from travel agents. Tourist information offices in Vienna (listed on page 122) can book rooms for you, for a small fee. Telephone assistance is available year-round through "Wien-Hotels," Tel. 211 14 444; fax 211 144 45, e-mail <rooms@info.wien.at>. If you do cancel your reservation, the hotel has a right to charge a cancellation fee. Nearly all establishments these days accept major credit cards.

The friendly atmosphere of a Pension in Vienna makes it popular for longer stays, though, as with some of the cheaper hotels, not all of them have rooms with private baths. It is always advisable to book ahead, especially for travel from Easter to the end of September, and at Christmas and New Year's. It is also possible to stay in private homes on a bed-and-breakfast basis. This is an especially attractive option in some of the smaller villages around Vienna (reservations through the tourist board's Wien-Hotels service). The famous old luxury hotels around the Opera are often fully booked by a long-established clientèle, so reservations are necessary well in advance. However "old fashioned" they may appear on the outside, Vienna's luxury hotels often have full, state-of-the-art business facilities, Internet access, in-room e-mail options, etc., as well as gym facilities, sauna, and steam bath.

a guest house	**eine Pension**
a single/double room	**ein Einzel-/Doppelzimmer**
with/without bath (shower)	**mit/ohne Bad (Dusche)**
What's the rate per night?	**Was kostet eine Übernachtung?**

AIRPORT *(Flughafen)*

Wien-Schwechat Airport, about 20 km (12 miles) from the center of Vienna, handles domestic and international flights. The modern building has a bank, restaurants, cafés, news and souvenir stands, a duty-free shop, and the Vienna Airport Tourist Information Office. For the 30-minute drive to the city center, beside the airport bus service (details see PUBLIC TRANSPORT, page 118), there are plenty of taxis, and a slower but more economical private shuttle service to take you to your exact address: Airport Service Mazur, counter at Arrivals level, Tel. 7007 64 22.

B

BICYCLE AND IN-LINE SKATE RENTALS *(Fahrrad/In-Line-Skater-Verleih)*

With the increase in bicycle lanes, both cycling and in-line skating are growing in popularity among tourists as well as local citizens as a way of beating the traffic snarls. The Ringstrasse makes a perfect circular route for seeing the sights, and the Wienerwald on the city outskirts has 230 km (over 140 miles) of cycle paths through the woods — for leisurely family excursions or mountain-bikers. Bicycle rentals are available at main-line railway stations and Csarmann *(6, Linke Wienzeile 124, Tel. 597 82 88)* rents both bikes and skates, and organizes guided tours for skaters (advance booking required).

BUDGETING FOR YOUR TRIP

To give you an idea of what to expect, here is a list of average prices in Austrian schillings (ÖS). They can only be approximate, however, as in Austria, too, inflation creeps relentlessly up. One way to save money is the new Vienna Card, available from the Tourist Office (see page 122) and providing substantial discounts or transportation, sightseeing, shopping, and entertainment.

Airport. Bus to center 70 ÖS, taxi 350–450 ÖS, train 35 ÖS.

Bicycle rent. 100–250 ÖS a day.

Car rent (advance booking from abroad, unlimited mileage, all insurance and taxes included) between 1,500–4,500 ÖS per day (3-day minimum) and 7,200–21,000 ÖS per week.

Entertainment. Cinema 70–100 ÖS, nightclub 400–500 ÖS, disco from 50 ÖS upwards.

Guides. 1,200 ÖS for half a day, 2,400 ÖS per day.

Hotels (double room with bath per night). ***** 1,700–6,800 ÖS, **** 1,200–3,000 ÖS, *** 800–1,800 ÖS, ** 650–1,200 ÖS, * 600–1,000 ÖS. (Categories ***** and **** include breakfast.)

Meals and drinks. Continental breakfast 60 ÖS, lunch/dinner in fairly good establishment 200–300 ÖS, coffee 25–35 ÖS, Austrian wine (bottle) 200–250 ÖS, cocktail 75–100 ÖS.

Museums. Entrance fees vary considerably. Concessions are available at many museums for holders of the Vienna Card. Entrance for children under six is free.

Public transport. 20 ÖS for single ticket, 17 ÖS single ticket bought in advance, 24-hour ticket 50 ÖS, 3-day ticket 135 ÖS.

Sightseeing. Fiaker 400 ÖS for a short tour, 800 ÖS for a longer one (but not that much longer!), MS Vindobona motorboat 140–245 ÖS.

Taxis. Meter starts at 24 ÖS, 11 ÖS per km or 4 ÖS per minute.

Tickets. Concerts 50–700 ÖS (standing 50 ÖS); opera 50–2,500 ÖS (wheelchair-places and companion 50 ÖS, standing 15–20 ÖS); Spanish Riding School training 80 ÖS, children 20 ÖS, shows 220–800 ÖS (standing 150–160 ÖS); Vienna Boys' Choir 60–250 ÖS (standing free).

C

CAMPING

Of camping sites located around the city, one is open all year round (except during February): Campingplatz der Stadt Wien, Wien West

II (Tel. 914 23 14). Other sites: Neue Donau (Tel./fax 220 93 10); Wien West I (Tel. 914 23 14); and Wien Süd (Tel. 865 92 18). They are very well organized.

CAR RENTAL/HIRE *(Autovermietung)*

For traveling inside the city, parking would make a car more of a hindrance than an asset, but having a car is certainly useful for excursions out to the Wienerwald and the Danube Valley. Though some local firms may offer lower prices than Avis, Budget, Europcar, and Hertz, these international agencies are more likely to let you return the car elsewhere in the country at no extra cost. Similar to those in other major European capitals, Vienna's prices average around 3,000 ÖS per day for a three-day rental. The best deal is through your travel agency before leaving home. Third-party insurance is compulsory, but full coverage is recommended. To avoid unpleasant surprises, make sure the price quoted includes all the necessary insurance and taxes.

To rent a car, you must show your driver's license (held for at least a year) and passport. You also need a major credit card, or a large deposit will be required. Minimum age for renting cars ranges from 20 to 23.

I'd like to rent a car (for today).   **Ich möchte (für heute) ein Auto mieten.**

CLIMATE

Spring is Vienna's most pleasant season. Chestnut trees and white lilacs are in blossom for the city's music festival. In July and August the Viennese leave the city relatively free for visitors, and in autumn, the Wienerwald is in splendid color for the Heuriger wine-gardens — and the opera and theater downtown. Even in winter Vienna is worth the trip for a marvelous white Christmas, in spite of the cold east wind.

The following chart shows Vienna's average monthly temperatures:

	J	F	M	A	M	J	J	A	S	O	N	D
°F	30	34	41	50	59	64	68	66	61	50	41	34
°C	-1	1	5	10	15	18	20	19	16	10	5	1

CLOTHING (*Kleidung*)

For the extremes of Vienna's weather, take light cottons for the very hot summer afternoons and your warmest woollens for the bitter winter. That wind off the steppes can whip through at any time; so even in summer, for an occasional cool evening, take a sweater and raincoat.

The Viennese like to dress up for the theater, concerts, and opera, but a dark suit or cocktail dress is nearly always appropriate. A tuxedo (dinner jacket) or evening dress may be worn on special occasions, such as premières and galas.

COMPLAINTS (*Reklamationen*)

Modern Vienna is remarkably efficient. But if something should go wrong, report the matter to the Vienna Tourist Board, listed under TOURIST INFORMATION. In hotels, restaurants, and shops, complaints should be addressed to the manager or proprietor. For more serious affairs, contact the police or your consulate.

CRIME AND SAFETY

Austria's crime and theft rate is quite low, compared to other parts of Europe. Nonetheless it is advisable not to leave valuable objects — especially cameras — in your car, which should always be left locked. If your passport is stolen, the police will give you a certificate to take to your consulate.

I want to report a theft. **Ich möchte einen Diebstahl melden.**

CUSTOMS (*Zoll*) AND ENTRY REQUIREMENTS

Only a valid passport is required for entry, just ID for member countries of the European Union (EU). As Austria is part of the EU, free exchange of non-duty free goods for personal use is permitted between Austria and the UK and Ireland. However, duty-free items may be subject to restrictions: Check with your travel agency or airline before going. For residents of non-EU countries, restrictions are as follows:

Australia: 200 cigarettes *or* 250 g tobacco *and* 1 liter alcohol

Canada: 200 cigarettes *and* 1 kg tobacco *and* 1.14 *l* alcohol

New Zealand: 200 cigarettes *or* 250 g tobacco *and* 1.1 *l* alcohol

South Africa: 200 cigarettes *and* 250 g tobacco *and* 1 *l* alcohol

USA: 200 cigarettes and a "reasonable quantity" of tobacco and 1 *l* alcohol.

Currency restrictions: Foreign and Austrian money can be taken into Austria without restriction. You can export 50,000 schillings in Austrian currency and an unlimited amount of foreign currency. Banks must report transactions of 100,000 schillings or more, in line with laws aimed at preventing money-laundering.

VAT reimbursement: For purchases of more than 1,000 schillings you can have the value-added tax *(Mehrwertsteuer)* reimbursed if you are taking the goods out of the EU. The salesperson fills out a form (called "U 34") with your home address, passport number, and the amount of the purchase. At the border a customs official will stamp this form, which you must then mail to the shop for reimbursement by check or bank-order.

I've nothing to declare.	**Ich habe nichts zu verzollen.**
It's for my personal use.	**Das ist für meinen persönlichen Gebrauch.**

D

DRIVING IN AUSTRIA
To bring your car into Austria you will need:

Valid driving license (national license for Europeans)

Car registration papers

National identity sticker for your car

Red warning triangle in case of breakdown

First-aid kit

For visitors who want to rent a car in Austria, see CAR RENTAL section.

Road conditions are by and large very good in Austria, only remote country roads are not paved.

Driving regulations. Drive on the right, pass on the left. Although drivers in Austria follow the same basic rules which apply in other countries that drive on the right, some rules might differ somewhat:

• you must wear seat-belts;

• children under the age of 12 may not sit in front, and must use a special safety seat;

• on the freeway *(Autobahn)* passing another vehicle on the right is prohibited;

• vehicles coming from the right have priority at crossroads without other signals;

• trams have priority, even when coming from the left;

• vehicles must halt behind trams when they are slowing down to stop and when loading or unloading passengers;

• it is prohibited to use your horn (day or night) in town;

• motorcyclists must wear crash helmets and use dipped headlights throughout the day.

• drunken driving is a very serious offense in Austria. The permissible alcohol level in the blood is 0.8%.

Speed limits. On motorways (expressways) 130 km/h (81 mph) or 100 km/h (62 mph); on other roads 100 km/h or 80 km/h (50 mph);

in built-up areas 50 km/h (31 mph); with caravan (trailer) 80 km/h on the open road; with studded tires 100 km/h on motorways, 80 km/h on other roads.

Parking. In streets with tram tracks, parking is prohibited from 8pm to 5am from mid-December to the end of March. If at all possible, use public transport within the Gürtel (outer ring road) since one-way streets and traffic jams add confusion within the city, where there's a real lack of parking space. To park in "blue" zones you'll need parking tickets, in use from 8am to 6pm for up to 90 minutes. Tickets are available in banks and tobacco shops (*Tabaktrafik*).

Breakdowns: Austrian automobile clubs offer 24-hour breakdown service to all drivers on motorways and main roads; ÖAMTC, Tel. 120; ARBÖ, Tel. 123.

Fuel and oil: There are plenty of stations, some of them self-service. In Vienna, most service stations close at night, but you can get fuel very late at highway entrances to the city.

Road signs: Most road signs employed in Austria are international pictographs but here are some written signs you might come across:

Anfang	(Parking) Start	**Ortsende**	Town ends
Ausfahrt	Exit	**Parken erlaubt**	Parking allowed
Aussicht	Viewpoint	**Rechts, links einbiegen**	Turn right, left
Bauarbeiten	Road works		
Einbahnstrasse	One way	**Rollsplitt**	Loose gravel
		Ende	(Parking) End
Sackgasse	Dead end street	**Fahrbahnwechsel**	Change lanes
Spital	Hospital		
Steinschlag	Falling stones	**Fussgänger**	Pedestrians
Umleitung	Diversion	**Gefahr**	Danger (detour)

Geradeaus	Straight on	**Vorfahrt**	Priority
Glatteis	Slippery roads	**Vorsicht**	Caution
Halten verboten	No stopping	**Werktags von 7 bis 17 Uhr**	Weekdays 7am to 5pm
Licht einschalten	Use headlights	**Zufahrt gestattet**	Entry permitted

driving license	**Führerschein**
car registration papers	**Zulassungsschein**
green card	**Grüne Karte**
Where's the nearest car park, please?	**Wo ist der nächste Parkplatz, bitte?**
Can I park here?	**Darf ich hier parken?**
Are we on the right road for...?	**Sind wir auf der richtigen Strasse nach...**
Check the oil/tires/battery, please.	**Öl/Reifen/Batterie prüfen, bitte.**
I've had a breakdown.	**Ich habe eine Panne.**
There's been an accident.	**Es ist ein Unfall passiert.**

Fluid measures

Distance

E

ELECTRIC CURRENT

You'll need an adapter for most British and US plugs: Austrian sockets have round holes. Supplies are 220 volt, and US equipment will require a transformer. Shaver outlets are generally dual voltage.

EMBASSIES AND CONSULATES

Contact your consulate or embassy only for real emergencies, such as loss of a passport or all your money, a serious accident or trouble with the police.

Australia Mattiellistrasse 2-4, 1040 Vienna. Tel. 512 85 80 1 64.

Canada Laurenzerberg 2, 1010 Vienna. Tel. 531 38 30 00.

Ireland Landstrasser Hauptstrasse 2, 1030 Vienna. Tel. 715 42 46 0.

New Zealand Springsiedelgasse 28, 1090 Vienna. Tel. 318 85 05, fax 377 66 0.

South Africa Sandgasse 33, 1190 Vienna. Tel. (embassy) 326 49 30; (consulate) 756 11 7.

UK Jauresgasse 12, 1030 Vienna. Tel. (embassy) 713 15 75; (consulate) 714 61 17.

US (embassy) Boltzmanngasse 16, 1090 Vienna.. Tel. 313 39; (consulate) Gartenbaupromenade 2, 1010 Vienna.

EMERGENCIES *(Notfälle)*

If your hotel receptionist isn't at hand, the Viennese telephone service has several emergency numbers. The most important ones are listed below. If you speak no German, try in English or find someone who speaks English to help you call. See also MEDICAL CARE.

Police emergency **133**

Fire **122**

Ambulance, first aid **144**

Pharmacist on duty **15 50**

Emergency medical service **141**

Emergency dentist **512 2078**

I need a doctor/dentist.	**Ich brauche einen Arzt/ Zahnarzt.**
ambulance	**Krankenwagen**
Fire!	**Feuer!**
Help!	**Hilfe!**
hospital	**Spital**
police	**Polizei**

G

GAY AND LESBIAN TRAVELERS

This sophisticated capital has a relatively friendly attitude toward gays and lesbians. Since 1996, their Regenbogen Parade (Rainbow Parade) is held every June on the Ringstrasse. A list of restaurants, hotels, bars, etc., which cater to gays and lesbians, is available in a privately published *"Gay City Map"* is available at some bars and hotels or directly from the publisher: BG Verlag, Mariahilferstrasse 123/3, 1060 Vienna. Two meeting places: Hosi Zentrum, *2, Novaragasse 40; Tel. 216 6604,* and Rosa Lila Villa, *6, Linke Wienzeile 102; Tel. 586 8150.*

GETTING THERE

Although the information below has been carefully checked, it is always advisable to consult a travel agent or local authority to verify the latest information on exact times, fares, and other arrangements.

By Air

Scheduled flights. There is regular service to Vienna from various centers in the UK. Flying time from London is two and a half hours.

In addition to non-stop flights from New York and Chicago, there is scheduled service from more than 40 American cities as well as a dozen cities in Canada to European gateway destinations from which you can make connections to Vienna.

Charter flights. Cheap charter flights are readily available from the UK. Accommodation is not generally included.

Charters are scheduled from a selection of North American cities, including ABC (Advanced Booking Charter) flights good for two-, three- and four-week stays, and OTC (One-Stop Inclusive Tour Charter) package deals which include round-trip air transport, hotel accommodation, selected meals, and sightseeing. In addition, dozens of American tour operators have individual and group packages to Austria offering stays of from two days to two weeks in Vienna. Consult a reputable travel agent for details of current programs.

By Car

The quickest route to Vienna from the UK is via Ostend through Brussels, Cologne, Nuremburg, Passau, and Linz, although there are more attractive routes, such as *die romantische Strasse* (the Romantic Road), via Rothenburg ob der Tauber, through the countryside. The ferry crossings to Ostend leave from Dover and Folkstone.

Depending on which direction you come from, you might be able to put your car on the train for part of the journey. In the summer a car-train *(Autozug)* service links Vienna with cities in Germany and Italy. Arriving with the car-train allows you to avoid traffic jams approaching Vienna and puts you near the center of town.

The Austrian Federal Railways runs car-trains between Vienna and Bischofshofen, Feldkirch (overnight service with couchettes also available), Linz, Villach, and Innsbruck and Salzburg (both during the skiing season only).

By Rail

The Ostend–Vienna express takes about 16 hours; the whole trip, London to Vienna, takes about 24 hours. Couchettes and sleepers are available, but must be reserved in advance.

Various special rail cards are valid for travel in Austria. The Inter-Rail Card allows unlimited travel across most of Europe and Morocco, and is available for a period of four weeks to travelers under 26. A cheaper zonal Inter-Rail Card is also available; Zone C covers Austria, Germany, Denmark, and Switzerland. The Euro Domino pass is valid for unlimited travel on any 3, 5, or 10 days within a one-month period, in the country or countries of your choice.

The free Rail-Europe-Senior ticket allows pensioners 30% reduction on travel in more than 20 European countries.

Visitors from outside Europe can buy a Eurailpass — a flat-rate, unlimited-mileage ticket good for first-class trains anywhere in Western Europe, including Great Britain. Eurail Youthpass offers second-class travel at a cheaper rate to anyone under 26. Passes are also available that allow unlimited travel for a specified period within Austria and a combination of selected other European countries.

The Austrian National Railpass (Bundes-Netzkarte) allows unlimited travel on Austrian Railways for one month. The regional "Puzzleticket" allows four days' travel on all railways during a period of ten days within one of four regions of Austria.

By Coach
Coach services connect many European cities and Vienna in summer. Overnight accommodation is usually added to the cost of the trip.

GUIDES AND TOURS (Fremdenführer; Rundfahrten)
The most romantic tour of Vienna is in the famous horse-drawn Fiaker cab. These are usually parked at the Heldenplatz, Stephansplatz, or near the Albertina and will take you around the major sightseeing spots — the younger ones may provide a running commentary in English as you ride. Make sure you agree on the cost of the trip before you begin. The price of a tram ticket will take you right round the Ringstrasse, but without commentary.

Vienna-Line bus tours, with an English-speaking hostess, are conveniently run on a hop-on/hop-off basis at 13 stops along the sightseeing route, starting out from the Staatsoper. An uninterrupted tour lasts 2 ¹/2 hours, but you can spread it over two days. Tickets in many hotels of from Vienna Sightseeing Tours, *3, Stelzhammergasse 4/11; Tel. 712 46 83 0.*

The Tourist Information Board organizes guided theme-tours on foot *(Wiener Spaziergänge)*, often with English-speaking guides.

Most hotels can arrange for English-speaking guides or interpreters. Or contact:

Travel Point *9, Boltzmanngasse 19. Tel. 319 42 43, fax 310 3875.*
Vienna Guide Service *19, Sommerhaidenweg 124. Tel. 440 3094 0, fax 440 2825.*

We'd like an English-speaking guide.	**Wir möchten einen englisch-sprachigen Fremdenführer.**
I need an English interpreter.	**Ich brauche einen Dolmetscher für Englisch.**
How long with the ride take?	**Wie lange dauert die Fahrt?**
What does it cost?	**Was kostet es?**

H

HEALTH AND MEDICAL CARE *(Ärztliche Hilfe)*
You should have few worries in Vienna. Its doctors are among the best in Europe and the tap (faucet) water is of course perfectly safe to drink. Ask your insurance company before leaving home if medical treatment in Austria is covered by your policy. Pack whatever prescription drugs you may need, as you may not find exactly the same in Vienna.

Most pharmacies *(Apotheke)* are open Monday to Friday and Saturday morning (see OPENING HOURS). For night and Sunday service, pharmacies display the address of the nearest shop remaining on duty. To find out which are open, Tel. **15 50**. (See also EMERGENCIES.)

| Where is there a pharmacy on duty? | **Wo ist die diensthabende Apotheke?** |

LANGUAGE

Austria is German-speaking, but English is also very widely understood and spoken. If you don't speak German, don't forget to ask *"Sprechen Sie Englisch?"* (Do you speak English?) before plunging ahead.

The *Berlitz German Phrase Book and Dictionary* covers most situations you're likely to encounter in Austria.

LAUNDRY AND DRY-CLEANING

Getting your clothes washed or cleaned by the hotel is fast and convenient, but prices are high. It is worth seeking out neighborhood dry-cleaners or self-service laundries. There are some laundries which offer same-day service. The *Gelbe Seiten* (Yellow Pages) list addresses under *Wäschereien* (laundries) and *Putzereien* (dry cleaners), or ask your hotel reception.

| When will it be ready? | **Wann ist es fertig?** |

| For tomorrow morning, please. | **Bis morgen früh, bitte.** |

LOST PROPERTY *(Fundamt)*

The city lost property office is at *Wasagasse 22. Tel. 313 44 92 11;* Mon–Fri, 8am–noon.

| I've lost my passport/ wallet/ handbag | **Ich habe meinen Pass/meine Brieftasche/Handtasche verloren.** |

MAPS

The Tourist Information Board gives away excellent street-maps of the city. Most useful will always be a large-scale map of the

Vienna

Innere Stadt (Inner City) and of the U-Bahn network. The one other place for which you will really need a map is the Kunsthistorisches (Fine Arts) Museum — you'll find them for free at the information desk.

MEDIA

Major hotels and most kiosks in the First District sell English-language daily newspapers from London, *International Herald Tribune*, *Wall Street Journal*, and *USA Today*, and the news magazines.

TV in the major hotels usually has CNN and BBC World news services, along with other major European channels. Shortwave radio enthusiasts can get BBC World Service and VOA — check appropriate wavelengths before leaving home. Blue Danube Radio (102.5 FM) broadcasts English- and French-language news and entertainment.

Vienna Tourist Board's *Monatsprogramm* provides full monthly cultural listings. German-speakers get a less formal, fresher view of the city's events, along with a full restaurant guide, with the first-rate monthly *Falter* magazine (similar to London's *Time Out* or New York's *Village Voice*).

MONEY MATTERS *(Geld)*

Austria's monetary unit is the *Schilling*, abbreviated ÖS, S, or Sch., divided into *Groschen* (abbreviated g.). Coins: 1, 5, 10, and 20 ÖS and 2, 5, 10, and 50 g. Be careful not to confuse the similar 5- and 10-Schilling coins. Bank-notes: 20, 50, 100, 500, and 1,000 and 5,000 ÖS.

Banks and currency exchange. Foreign currency can be changed in practically all banks and savings banks (*Sparkasse*). You can also change money at travel agencies and hotels, but the rate will not be as good (see OPENING HOURS.) Fastest is with your bank card at the now ubiquitous automatic cash distributors. Major credit cards are accepted in almost all hotels, most restaurants and most shops in the tourist neighborhoods.

114

Some exchange offices are open on weekends, including those at the airport, Südbahnhof, Westbahnhof, Air Terminal, Stephansplatz, and Opernpassage. They're open from early morning (some from 6:30am) until late afternoon or evening every day of the week. Note that all post offices cash Eurocheques.

Money-changing machines (CHANGE) that will take US$5, $10, and $20 notes are to be found at Stephansplatz 2 (near Stephansdom); Kärntnerstrasse 32, 43, and 51; Operngasse 8 (next to the Opera); Graben 21; Michaelerplatz 3; Schottenring 1; Tegetthoffstrasse 7; Franz-Josefs-Kai 1; and Schloss Schönbrunn.

Traveler's checks *(Reisescheck)* are welcome almost everywhere; but, again, the rates are best in banks or exchange offices.

I want to change some pounds/dollars	**Ich möchte Pfund/ Dollar wechseln.**
Do you accept traveler's checks?	**Nehmen Sie Reisechecks an?**
Do you have any change, please?	**Haben Sie Kleingeld, bitte?**

OPENING HOURS

Shops. Most small places are open from 9am (grocery stores an hour earlier) to 6pm with a break for lunch. Major department stores do business 8am–6pm non-stop, but supermarkets close for about two hours at lunch. Most shops close Saturday afternoon, though some stay open until 5pm on the first Saturday of each month. Shops in railway stations are open daily 7am–11pm. (New legislation may soon extend shopping hours.)

Museums. Hours vary considerably (see individual listings under *Museums*, page 51, and *Other Museums*, page 60.

Banks. Mon–Fri 8am–3pm (Thu to 5:30pm). Most branches close 12:30–1:30pm.

Vienna

Post offices Mon–Fri 8am–6pm. For 24-hour service, see POST OFFICE.

Pharmacies Mon–Fri 8am–noon, 2–6pm; Sat 8am–noon.

P

POLICE *(Polizei)*

Vienna's police wear green caps and jackets with black trousers, and drive white cars. Traffic police wear white caps and, in summer, white jackets. Street parking is supervised by *"Politessen"* (meter-maids) in blue jackets and white hats. Police on motorcycles are popularly known as "white mice" *(weisse Mäuse)*. If you are fined for any reason, the police have the right to ask you to pay on the spot.

In emergencies, call **133**.

Where is the nearest police station, please?	**Wo ist die nächste Polizei-wachstube, bitte?**

POST OFFICE *(Postamt)*

Apart from regular post office hours, post offices at main railway stations (Westbahnhof, Südbahnhof, and Franz Josefs-Bahnhof) are open day and night. Other offices offering this 24-hour service for registered, air, and express mail (with a small extra charge for after-hours service): Central Post Office, Fleischmarkt 19 and Central Telegraph Office, Börseplatz 1.

Stamps are also available at tobacco shops *(Tabaktrafik).*

Fax. Many post offices have fax services both for sending and receiving correspondence. Central Post Office fax: 535 3518.

Telegrams. Minimum for a regular telegram is seven words. *Brieftelegramm* (Night Letters) are transmitted as a telegram and delivered with the normal mail of the day. Per-word costs are half the price of the regular telegram rate (minimum 22 words).

express (special delivery)	**Express/Eilbote**
airmail	**Luftpost**

Have you any mail for...?	**Haben Sie Post für...?**
A stamp for this letter/ post card, please.	**Eine Marke für diesen Brief/ diese Postkarte, bitte.**
I want to fax a letter to...	**Ich möchte einen Brief nach... faxen.**

PUBLIC HOLIDAYS (Feiertage)

Austria observes 14 public holidays a year on which banks, museums, official services, and many restaurants are closed. On Good Friday, a holiday for Protestants only, shops remain open.

January 1	Neujahrstag	New Year's Day
January 6	Heilige Drei Könige	Twelfth Night
May 1	Staatsfeiertag (Tag der Arbeit)	Labor Day
August 15	Mariä Himmelfahrt	Assumption
October 26	Nationalfeiertag (Tag der Fahne)	National Holiday (Flag Day)
November 1	Allerheiligen	All Saints' Day
December 8	Unbefleckte Empfängnis	Immaculate Conception
December 25	Weihnachten	Christmas Day
December 26	Stefanstag	St. Stephen's Day

Movable dates:

Karfreitag	Good Friday
Ostermontag	Easter Monday
Christi Himmelfahrt	Ascension Day
Pfingstmontag	Whit Monday
Fronleichnam	Corpus Christi

Vienna

On 24 December (Christmas Eve) theaters and cinemas are closed all day and shops, restaurants, and coffee houses close at midday.

Are you open tomorrow?   **Haben Sie morgen geöffnet?**

PUBLIC TRANSPORT

Maps for buses, trams, and U-Bahn (subway) are available at main stops as well as at the central public transport information offices at Karlsplatz and Stephansplatz.

Tickets can be bought from a conductor or a machine on trams and buses, from booking office or machine for mainline or city trains. There are different types of tickets available; flat rate for tram, train, subway, and all bus services is good for changes made without interruption. Discount tickets can be bought in advance from a tobacconist's *(Tabaktrafik)* or transport offices *(Verkehrsbetriebe)*. Travel passes are available for 24 hours, 3 days, and 8 days. Also worth considering is the Vienna Card, a 72-hour ticket currently costing 180 ÖS, valid on all public transport and entitles holder to discounts at concerts and museums.

Trams *(Strassenbahn)*: With some 35 tram routes, this is Vienna's most important form of public transport. On most trams (and buses) the driver serves as the conductor. These vehicles carry a blue sign front and rear with the word *"Schaffnerlos"* (without conductor). If you have a ticket, enter by the door marked *Entwerter* and have it stamped; otherwise get in at the front and buy your ticket from the vending machine. For trams with conductors, enter at the rear to buy a ticket or have it stamped.

Buses: The airport bus service runs between the city air terminal at Landstrasser Hauptstrasse (Hilton Hotel) and the airport every 20 or 30 minutes. Count on a half hour for the ride.

U-Bahn (subway): Five lines operate at present, covering all the main parts of town. Tickets can be purchased from machines or ticket offices.

Schnellbahn (rapid-transit): Suburban trains depart from the Südbahnhof for outlying districts. The unit fare applies in the central zone, standard fares outside. Other points of departure are Wien Nord and Wien Mitte.

R

RELIGION
Austria is predominantly Roman Catholic. Sunday mass in some churches is accompanied by orchestral and choral works. Consult a newspaper under "Kirchenmusik" for exact times.

English-language Catholic mass is held at 11am at Votivkirche, Rooseveltplatz 8, Tel. 408 5050 14. There is an Anglican/Episcopal Church at Jauresgasse 17–19, Tel. 720 7973.

Jewish services take place at the Stadttempel, Seitenstettengasse 4, tel. 531 0415.

T

TAXIS
As in any big city, Vienna never has enough taxis at rush hour, so book in advance through your hotel receptionist or by calling one of the following numbers: Tel. 31 300; 40 100; 60 160; or 91 011. If you want to go beyond the city limits, negotiate the fare in advance.

TELEPHONES
Austria's country code is **43**, Vienna's area code is **(0)1**, dropping the 0 for calls from abroad. For **international calls** from Vienna, dial **00** before the country code (**1** for US, **44** for UK, etc.), then the area code and number of your destination.

Long-distance and international calls can be made from any phone box, but if you need assistance, you can call from post offices or your hotel (and pay a supplement). Hotel charges are often double the public phone rates. As an alternative to coins, more and more phone boxes take a phone card *(Telefonwertkarte)* available at post offices and tobacconists.

The booths all have multilingual instructions. Calls are cheaper 6pm–8am and Saturdays, Sundays, and public holidays.

Information operator for Austria: 16 11

Information operator for Germany: 16 12

Information operator for rest of Europe: 16 13

Information operator for rest of world: 16 14

Operator for abroad (to reverse charges): 09

TICKETS *(Karten)*

Tickets for performances can be obtained at private ticket agencies *(Theaterkartenbüro)* all over the city, as well as at major hotels, but these will cost at least 22 percent more. Try Vienna Ticket Service, *1043 Vienna, Postfach 160. Tel. 587 98 43, fax 587 98 44.*

Concerts. Tickets are usually sold by subscription, and are rarely available at the box office or by post. To book the occasional seat on sale to the public contact: Wiener Philharmoniker, *Bösendorferstrasse 12, 1010 Vienna,* or Musikalische Jugend, same address as above.

Spanish Riding School. Written orders for tickets are essential and should be sent at least six months in advance to: Spanische Reitschule, *Hofburg, 1010 Vienna.* Tickets can be bought on the day for the morning training sessions.

Opera and Theater. The best place for opera tickets is the national theater ticket office *(Österreichischer Bundestheaterverband, Bestellbüro).* They sell tickets seven days ahead for opera (Staatsoper), operetta (Volksoper), Burgtheater, and Akademietheater performances (closed in July and August); you can reserve tickets at least 3 weeks before the performance by writing to the same address: Bundestheaterkassen, *Goethegasse 1, 1010 Vienna.* For information the number to call is 514 44 29 59 or 514 44 29 60. Ticket sales by credit card are available six days in advance. Tel. 513 1513 or fax 514 44 2969. Standing-room tickets are sold for evening performances, at the box office prior to the performance.

Vienna Boys' Choir (Wiener Sängerknaben). Obtain tickets in advance at the Hofburg Kapelle on Fridays 5–7pm for Sunday performances, or reserve at least two months in advance from: Hofmusikkapelle, *Hofburg, Schweizerhof, 1010 Vienna.*

The choir can also be heard every Friday at the Konzerthaus in May, June, September, and October. Tickets are available from major hotels, or Reisebüro Mondial, *Faulmanngasse 4, 1040 Vienna.*

TIME ZONES

Austria is on Central European Time (GMT+1). In summer, clocks move ahead one hour, and the time difference looks like this:

New York	London	**Vienna**	Jo'burg	Sydney	Auckland
6am	11am	**noon**	noon	8pm	10pm

TIPPING

Since a service charge is included in hotel and restaurant bills, tipping is not obligatory. However, it's appropriate to give something extra to porters, cloakroom attendants, hotel maids, etc., for their services. The chart below makes some suggestions as to how much to leave.

Hotel porter, per bag	20 ÖS
Maid, per week	50 ÖS
Waiter	5% (optional)
Lavatory attendant	10 ÖS
Taxi driver	round off fare
Tour guide	10%
Barber/Hairdresser	10–15%
Theater usher	10 ÖS

TOILETS *(Toiletten)*

Public facilities can be found near important streets or squares, often in the pedestrian underpasses. Normally toilets in cafés can be used without ordering anything but it's always more courteous to have a coffee or a beer. If hand towels and soap are used in public facilities, there is often a set fee rather than just tip. Have a couple of Schilling ready in case the door has a "slot" machine.

Toilets may be labeled with male or female pictograms, WC, or *Damen* (Ladies) and *Herren* (Gentlemen).

TOURIST INFORMATION

The Austrian National Tourist Office *(Österreichische Fremden-verkehrswerbung)* has comprehensive information about what to see, when to go, and where to stay in and around Vienna.

Australia: ANTO, 1st Floor, 36 Carrington Street, Sydney NSW 2000. Tel. (2) 299-3621, fax 299-3808.

Canada: ANTO, 2 Bloor Street East, Suite 3330, Toronto, Ontario M4W 1A8. Tel. (416) 967-3381, fax (416) 967-4101.

Ireland: ANTO, Merrion Hall, Strand Road, Sandymount, PO Box 2506, Dublin 4. Tel. (01) 283-0488, fax (01) 283-0531.

South Africa: ANTO, Cradock Heights, 21 Cradock Avenue, Rosebank, 2196 Johannesburg. Tel. (11) 442-7235, fax (11) 442-8304.

UK: ANTO, 30 St. George Street, London W1R OAL. Tel. (0171) 629-0461, fax (0171) 499-6038.

US: ANTO, PO Box 1142, New York, NY 10108-1142. Tel. (212) 944-6880, fax (212) 730-4568.

ANTO, PO Box 491938, Los Angeles, CA 90045. Tel. (310) 477-3332, fax (310) 477-5141.

Vienna Tourist Board

(Wiener Fremdenverkehrsverband), Obere Augartenstrasse 40, 1025 Vienna. Tel. (1) 211 140, fax (1) 216 8492, Mon–Fri

Recommended Hotels

Vienna's hotels compare in quality to those of other major European capitals. However, shortage of accommodation, particularly during peak season — Christmas and New Year, and from Easter to the end of September — does mean that booking is advisable. Reservations may be made by telephone, fax, or letter, and are binding even if not confirmed in writing.

Our guide follows the star classification system used by the Vienna Tourist Board. Categories of hotel — Hotel, Pension (guest-house), and Saison-Hotel (student hostel) — each have different requirements determining the number of stars they are awarded, which means that one category is not comparable with another even when both have the same number of stars. The following ranges give an idea of the price for a double room, per night, with private bath unless otherwise stated. A service charge and taxes are included in the price, unless otherwise stated. Breakfast is also usually included, most often a buffet of various cold meats and cheeses, cereals, bread, rolls, jam, and coffee. Always confirm prices when booking.

For more hotels, see the Vienna Tourist Board's free brochure *Hotels & Pensionen*, available at tourist information offices and travel agencies. Wien-Hotels is the tourist board's reservation service: Tel. 21114, ext. 444; fax 211 14 445; e-mail <rooms@info.wien.at>. For your own telephoning or faxing from abroad, country code is **43** followed by Vienna area code **1**. The district number precedes the street address.

$$$$$	over 3,500 ÖS
$$$$	2,500 ÖS–3,500 ÖS
$$$	1,600 ÖS–2,500 ÖS
$$	1,600 ÖS–1000 ÖS
$	under 1000 ÖS

All the hotels listed take major credit cards; wheelchair access where specified.

Vienna

Academia $$ *8, Pfeilgasse 3a; Tel. 401 76 48; fax 401 76 20.* A huge student hostel with restaurant in a fun area, just a short tram ride from the First District. 368 rooms.

Alexander $$$ *9, Augasse 15; Tel. 317 15 08; fax 317 15 08 82.* Extremely convenient if you intend to take trains to the north (e.g., Prague and Berlin). 54 rooms.

Am Brillantengrund $$$ *7, Bandgasse 4; Tel. 523 36 62; fax 526 13 30.* Family-run hotel pleasantly decorated in reproduction Biedermeier. 31 rooms.

Am Schubertring $$$$ *1, Schubertring 11; Tel. 717 020; fax 713 99 66.* Stylishly furnished 19th-century mansion conveniently located between Musikverein concert hall and Stadtpark. 39 rooms.

Amarante $$$ *5, Matzleinsdorferplatz 1; Tel. 544 27 43; fax 544 27 4380.* A typical 1950s Viennese building on the Margareten Gürtel (the southern ring road). Efficiently run, renovated with air conditioning. Wheelchair access. 43 rooms.

Ambassador $$$$$ *1, Neuer Markt 5; Tel. 514 66; fax 513 29 99.* A traditional Viennese hotel with a prime location on Kärntnerstrasse. It also offers a first-rate restaurant. 105 rooms.

ANA Grand Hotel $$$$$ *1, Kärntner Ring 9; Tel. 515 800; fax 515 13 13.* One of the city's old-world institutions resurrected in 1994 as a modern luxury hotel, with elegant shopping mall. 205 rooms.

Ananas $$$$ *5, Rechte Wienzeile 93-95; Tel. 546 20 0; fax 545 42 42.* Distinctively Viennese Jugendstil exterior; inside a very pleasant modern hotel. Wheelchair access. 537 rooms.

Arcotel Boltzmann $$$ *9, Boltzmanngasse 8; Tel. 316 12; fax 316 12 816.* Pleasant, modern hotel near the Modern Art Museum. 70 rooms.

Atlas $$$ *7, Lerchenfelderstrasse 1-3; Tel. 401 76 55; fax 401 76 20.* This student hostel is situated in one of the liveliest parts of the city, close to First District. 182 rooms.

Avis $$ *8, Pfeilgasse 4; Tel. 401 74; fax 40176 20.* Just opposite the Academia (listed above) and only a short walk away from a frequent tram service to the First District. 72 rooms.

Bristol $$$$$ *1, Kärntner Ring 1; Tel. 515 16 0; fax 515 16 55 0.* Old-fashioned stately establishment on the Ringstrasse, the Bristol rates among the great hotels of the world. 142 rooms.

Clima Cityhotel $$$ *4, Theresianumgasse 21a; Tel. 505 16 96; fax 504 35 52.* Functional modern hotel in same group as the Clima Villenhotel (listed below) with good standard of service. 39 rooms.

Clima Villenhotel $$$$ *19, Nussberggasse 2c; Tel. 371 51 6; fax 371 39 2.* A charming hotel located among the vineyards of the Wienerwald (Vienna Woods). Situated 7 km (4 miles) north of the city center in Nussdorf. 30 rooms.

De France $$$$$ *1, Schottenring 3; Tel. 313 68 0; fax 319 59 69.* Another of Vienna's smart Ringstrasse hotels in a convenient location for both business executive and tourist. 216 rooms.

Drei Kronen $$$ *4, Schleifmühlgasse 25; Tel. 587 32 89; fax 587 32 89 11.* Conveniently situated in the vicinity of the Naschmarkt, Vienna's best-known and largest market. 41 rooms.

Vienna

Europa $$$$ *1, Kärntner Strasse 18; Tel.h 515 94 0; fax 513 81 38.* Clean, modern, and in an excellent location for city centre sightseeing. 102 rooms

Gartenhotel Glanzing $$$$ *19, Glanzinggasse 23; Tel. 470 42 72 0; fax 470 42 72 14.* Located in one of Vienna's smartest residential districts, this family-run hotel is particularly welcoming to children, and has a garden where they are free to play. 18 rooms.

Hilton Vienna $$$$$ *3, Am Stadtpark; Tel. 717 00 0; fax 713 06 91.* Centrally located on the north edge of the Stadtpark next door to the City Air Terminal. 600 rooms.

Ibis Wien $$$ *6, Mariahilfer Gürtel 22-24; Tel. 599 98; fax 597 90 90.* Clean, comfortable, French chain hotel. Wheelchair access. 341 rooms.

Im Palais Schwarzenberg $$$$$ *3, Hotel im Palais Schwarzenberg, Schwarzenbergplatz 9; Tel. 798 45 15; fax 7984714.* Housed in an imposing Baroque palace, this is one of Vienna's most exclusive hotels. Delightful gardens and one of Vienna's finest restaurants (see page 136). 44 rooms.

Imperial $$$$$ *1, Kärntnerring 16; Tel. 501 10 0; fax 501 10 41 0.* Opened in 1873 by Emperor Franz Joseph, this is the city's favored celebrity hotel. Its Imperial Torte is a rival to Sacher's. 128 rooms.

Inter-Continental Wien $$$$$ *3, Johannesgasse 28; Tel. 711 22 0; fax 713 44 89.* Part of the American chain, this huge luxury hotel near the Stadtpark offers ultra-modern services. 492 rooms.

Jäger \$\$\$\$ *17, Hernalser Hauptstrasse 187; Tel. 486 66 20 0; fax 486 66 20 8.* A 4-star family-run hotel at an exceptionally low price, in a good shopping street. 18 rooms.

K & K Palais Hotel \$\$\$\$ *1, Rudolfsplatz 11; Tel. 533 13 53; fax 533 13 53 70.* Originally the town-house of famous actress Katharina Schratt, mistress of Emperor Franz Joseph. Wheelchair access. 66 rooms.

Kaiser Franz Josef A \$\$\$\$ *19, Sieveringerstrasse 4 - 10; Tel. 327 35; fax 327 35 5.* Attractive modern hotel in a quiet residential area, not too far from major attractions. Wheelchair access. 93 rooms.

Kaiserin Elisabeth \$\$\$\$ *1, Weihburgggasse 3; Tel. 515 260; fax 515 267.* Historic building (1809), favorite with composers Liszt, Wagner and their aristocratic friends. Grand Biedermeier furniture, Persian carpets. 53 rooms.

Kaiserpark Schönbrunn \$\$\$\$ *12, Grünbergstrasse 11; Tel. 81386 10 0; fax 8138183.* Pleasant, old-fashioned, family-run hotel offering a traditional Viennese atmosphere near Schönbrunn palace. Wheelchair access. 49 rooms.

Kärntnerhof \$\$\$ *1, Grashofgasse 4; Tel. 512 19 23; fax 513 22 28 33.* Attractive old building in a lively area of the First District, but in a quiet cul-de-sac. Wheelchair access. 43 rooms, some without bath.

Karolinenhof \$\$\$ *21, Jedleseerstrasse 75; Tel. 278 78 01; fax 278 78 01 8.* Rare hotel located in trans-Danube Vienna, ideal for families wanting to enjoy Donauinsel swimming. Wheelchair access. 49 rooms.

Vienna

König von Ungarn $$$$ *1, Schulerstrasse 10; Tel. 515 84 0; fax 515 84 8*. Charming mansion dating back to the 16th century on a quiet street near Stephansdom. Take breakfast in the pretty winter garden. 25 rooms.

Mailbergerhof $$$$ *1, Annagasse 7; Tel. 512 06 41; fax 512 06 4110*. Enjoy the personal touch of this family-run hotel in Baroque town-palace, nicely furnished, delightful inner courtyard. 40 rooms.

Nordbahn $$$ *2, Praterstrasse 72; Tel. 211 30 0; fax 211 30 72*. A comfortable, middle-class hotel near Prater park. The birthplace of Max Steiner, composer of the music for *Casablanca* and *Gone with the Wind*. Wheelchair access. 80 rooms.

Novotel Wien Airport $$$ *Flughafen Schwechat; Tel. 701 07; fax 707 32 39*. A comfortable, surprisingly friendly airport hotel conveniently situated close to the terminal. Wheelchair access. 180 rooms.

Papageno $$$ *4, Wiedner Hauptstrasse 23-25; Tel. 504 67 44; fax 504 67 44 22*. Friendly family hotel well located near the Karlsplatz. 39 rooms.

Parkhotel Schönbrunn $$$$ *13, Hietzinger Hauptstrasse 10–20; Tel. 878 04; fax 878 04 32 20*. Originally built as Emperor Franz Joseph's guesthouse, Vienna's largest hotel faces the main entrance of the Schloss Schönbrunn. 434 rooms.

Pension Dr. Geissler $$$ *1, Postgasse 14; Tel. 533 28 0; fax 533 26 35*. Clean and pleasant pension conveniently situated in the First District, with restaurant. 23 rooms, some without bath. Major credit cards.

Pension Kraml $$ *6, Brauergasse 5; Tel. 587 85 88; fax 586 75 73.* Family-run pension. Clean, comfortable, and friendly. 14 rooms, some without bath.

Pension Neuer Markt $$$$ *1, Seilergasse 9; Tel. 512 23 16; fax 513 91 05.* A pleasant pension with restaurant, adjacent to historic square. 37 rooms. Major credit cards.

Pension Pertschy $$$$ *1, Habsburgergasse 5; Tel. 534 490; fax 534 49 49.* Much sought after, in the heart of the antiques dealers' quarter. Wheelchair access. 47 rooms. Major credit cards.

Pension Residenz $$$ *1, Ebendorferstrasse 10; Tel. 4064786 0; fax 406 47 86 50.* An excellent position between the Rathaus (Town Hall) and the Ringstrasse university buildings. Wheelchair access. 15 rooms. Major credit cards.

Radisson SAS Palais Hotel $$$$$ *1, Parkring 16; Tel. 515 17 0; fax 512 22 16.* An Imperial-style hotel housed in one of the palaces on the Ringstrasse. This is one of the most expensive hotels in Vienna. 246 rooms.

Regina $$$$ *9, Rooseveltplatz 15; Tel. 404 46 0; fax 408 83 92.* Hotel from the early 1900s, situated next to Votivkirche with a large restaurant serving local specialties. Wheelchair access. 126 rooms.

Rogner Hotel Biedermeier im Sünnhof $$$$ *3, Landstrasse Hauptstrasse 28; Tel. 71671 0; fax 716 71 50 3.* Sprawling 19th-century house redolent with Old World charm. Excellent value for money. 203 rooms.

Sacher $$$$$ *1, Philharmonikerstrasse 4; Tel. 514 56; fax 514 57 81 0.* Vienna's most elegant and prestigious hotel is a *fin* *de siècle* gem. Its biggest claim to fame, though, is its chocolate cake, the Sachertorte (see page 96). 108 rooms.

Savoy $$$ *7, Lindengasse 12; Tel. 523 46 46; fax 523 46 40.* A comfortable hotel furnished with reproduction antique furniture. At this price level, one of the city's most agreeable bargains. 43 rooms.

Schlosshotel Wilhelminenberg $$$ *16, Savoyenstrasse 2; Tel. 485 85 030; fax 485 48 76.* Once home of the Vienna Boys' Choir, this splendid building with large garden overlooks city from the edge of Wienerwald (Vienna Woods). 87 rooms.

Tourotel Mariahilfer Strasse $$$ *15, Mariahilferstrasse 156; Tel. 892 33 35; fax 892 32 21 49 5.* A period building on a popular shopping street. Wheelchair access. 48 rooms.

Vienna Marriott Hotel $$$$$ *1, Parkring 12a; Tel. 515 180; fax 515 18 6736.* Part of a large American chain catering to the business traveler, the Marriott is situated on the Ringstrasse opposite the Stadtpark. Built in dramatic post-modern style. 313 rooms.

Wandl $$$ *1, Petersplatz 9; Tel. 534 55; fax 534 55 77.* A medieval building situated just off First District's Graben, this hotel was once a monastery and then (but no longer) a prostitutes' dormitory. Wheelchair access. 138 rooms, some without bath.

Zur Wiener Staatsoper $$$ *1, Krugerstrasse 11; Tel. 513 12 74; fax 513 12 74 15.* A pleasant family-run hotel right by the Opera. 22 rooms.

Recommended Restaurants

Dining out has always been a popular pastime in Vienna. It is part of Austrian culture to take the family out for lunch on the weekend, and to meet friends in a *Beisl* (convivial Viennese equivalent of the bistro) or at the *Heuriger* wine garden. In restaurants, the emphasis is on good company, good wine, robust portions, and usually, reasonable prices — a dramatically different approach from many other European capitals.

When choosing a restaurant, something to bear in mind during the summer months is whether you can sit outside in a garden or *Schanigarten* (tables on the pavement sheltered from the sun by sunshades).

If you're simply after a quick snack, then look for a Würstelstand, a small kiosk selling sausages and other local specialties, such as *Leberkäsesemmel* (liver pâté sandwich). These kiosks are to be found on street corners all over the city.

A recent, but by no means exhaustive, guide to Viennese restaurants lists nearly 4,000 restaurants, *Beisln*, cafés, etc., so what follows is a comparatively limited selection. Restaurants are listed alphabetically within the following price ranges:

$$$	500 ÖS–1000 ÖS
$$	200 ÖS–500 ÖS
$	200 ÖS and under

Price categories are based on the cost, per person, of a dinner comprising starter, mid-priced main course, and dessert (not including wine, coffee, or service). Heuriger, Stadtheuriger, and cafés are listed separately on pages 140–141. All serve meals in the above **$** category unless otherwise specified. See also the section on *Eating Out*, pages 91-97. Unless otherwise specified, lunch is served 12pm–3pm. Dinner service may start as early as 6pm (for theater-, opera- and concert-goers) and go on to midnight or later. Some kitchens stop one hour before closing time — check when making reservation. Major credit cards accepted unless otherwise specified.

Vienna

Achilleus $ *1, Köllnerhofgasse 3; Tel. 512 83 28*. Tucked away in a small side street in the "Bermuda Triangle" area of Vienna, this is one of the city's best Greek restaurants, prices reasonable, service exceptionally friendly. Open Mon–Fri dinner only, 5:30pm–midnight; Sat/Sun also lunch 11:30am–3pm, dinner 5:30pm–midnight.

Alte Taverne $ *7, Lindengasse 3; Tel. 523 4723*. Simple setting for simple fare, good value for money. Open Mon–Fri 11am–midnight, Sat/Sun 5pm–midnight.

Altwienerhof $$$ *15, Herklotzgasse 6; Tel. 892 60 00*. Highly acclaimed Central European cuisine with monumental wine cellar. Definitely worth the pilgrimage to the 15th District. Open Mon–Fri noon–2pm, dinner 6:30pm–2am.

Anna Sacher $$$ *1, Philharmonikerstrasse 4; Tel. 514 56 0*. In the monumental hotel, one of Vienna's top restaurants, renowned not only for its Sachertorte chocolate cake. Daily lunch; dinner 6pm–11:30pm.

Bier-Oase $ *9, Liechtensteinstrasse 108; Tel. 319 75 51*. With its solid Viennese fare, the restaurant offers around 120 types of beer. *Schanigarten*. Mon–Fri 10am–midnight, Sat 6pm–midnight, Sun closed.

Bodega Manchega $$ *9, Wasserburgergasse 2; Tel. 319 65 75*. Good Spanish and Mexican specialities. Enjoyable atmosphere with live music every evening. Daily lunch 11:30am–3pm, dinner 6:30pm–1am.

Brezelg'wölb $ *1, Ledererhof 9; Tel. 533 88 11*. A good selection of Austrian specialties in former baker's shop with Baroque

Palatschinkenkuchl $ *1, Köllnerhofgasse 4; Tel. 512 31 05*. Unpretentious, student atmosphere. Serves a variety of sweet and savory pancakes. Daily 10am–midnight.

Plachutta $$$ *1, Wollzeile 38; Tel. 512 15 77*. Exquisite service for definitive *haute cuisine* versions of Viennese specialities, especially a Tafelspitz fit for an emperor. Daily non-stop 11:30am–11:15pm.

Salzamt $$ *1, Ruprechtsplatz 1; Tel. 533 53 32*. A trendy bar/restaurant in Hermann Czech's stylish décor, frequented by writers, artists, and night-owls. Sophisticated treatment of old imperial delicacies. Daily dinner only 5pm–12:30am, bar till 4am.

Schnattl $$ *8, Lange Gasse 40; Tel. 405 34 0 0*. Good food and pleasant service in an area that is fast becoming a second center for Viennese restaurants. Excellent wine list. Open Mon–Fri 11:30am–2:30pm, 6pm–10pm; Sat/Sun dinner only 6pm–10pm.

Shalimar $ *6, Schmalzhofgasse 11; Tel. 596 43 17*. Vienna has only about a dozen Indian and Pakistani restaurants; this is one of the best. Daily noon–2:30pm, dinner 6pm–11pm.

Stadtbeisl $$ *1, Naglergasse 21; Tel. 533 35 07*. Old-fashioned interior with beautiful dark wood paneling. Large range of reasonably priced Viennese dishes. *Schanigarten*. Daily 10am–midnight.

Steirereck $$$ *3, Rasumofskygasse 2; Tel. 713 31 68*. Topnotch restaurant serving *Neue Wiener Küche* (Viennese nouvelle cuisine). Conservatory and pavement dining. *Wiener*

Vienna

Gabelfrühstück ("elevenses") served from 10:30am. Open Mon–Fri, lunch noon–2pm, dinner 7pm–midnight.

Trzesniewski $ *1, Dorotheergasse 1; Tel. 512 32 91.* Vienna's most famous sandwich bar, despite the uninviting exterior and unpronounceable name. No credit cards. 8:30am–7:30pm.

Vier Jahreszeiten $$$ *3, Johannesgasse 28; Tel. 711 22 14 3.* Inter-Continental Wien hotel's recently renovated Vier Jahreszeiten (Four Seasons) popular both with business executive and theater-goers. Open Mon–Fri lunch; dinner 7pm–midnight.

Weincomptoire $$ *1, Bäckerstrasse 6; Tel. 512 17 60.* As well as enjoying a selection of Viennese and other specialties, you can sample over 30 different wines by the glass, and a lot more by the bottle. Open Mon–Sat lunch; dinner 5pm–2am.

Zur Goldenen Glocke $$ *5, Kettenbrückengasse 8; Tel. 587 57 67.* Good, traditional Viennese cuisine at moderate prices, fresh produce from nearby Naschmarkt. Popular garden. Open Mon–Sat 11am–2:30pm, dinner 5:30pm–midnight.

Heuriger

10er Marie *16, Ottakringer Strasse 224; Tel. 409 4647.* A very old, very famous, and now very fashionable Heuriger. Popular hang-out amongst Viennese VIPs. Full menu. Year-round 3pm–midnight.

Bach-Hengl *19, Sandgasse 7, Grinzing; Tel. 320 24 39.* Family has been in business since 1137! Wine and meals in small and large rooms, children's playground. Year-round, 4pm–midnight.

décor. Romantic candlelight and sturdy old wooden tables and benches add to Old World atmosphere. Daily 11:30am–1am.

Da Conte $$$ *1, Kurrentgasse 12; Tel. 533 64 64 0*. Elegant restaurant specializing in Italian cuisine, reputed for its fresh seafood, flown in daily from Mediterranean. Mon–Sat lunch, dinner 6:30pm–1am.

Do & Co $$ *1, Stephansplatz 12; Tel. 535 39 69/18*. The magnificent cathedral view from the 7th floor of the Haas-Haus is worth the price, but you should not be disappointed by the refined cuisine, both traditional Viennese and international. Daily lunch, dinner 6pm–midnight.

Drei Husaren $$$ *1, Weihburggasse 4; Tel. 512 10 92*. Elegant restaurant serving beautifully prepared traditional Viennese cuisine with romantic piano accompaniment. The place to go for an evening of gracious living. Interesting and varied selection of starters. Daily lunch, dinner 6pm–1am.

Figlmüller $ *1, Wollzeile 5; Tel. 512 61 77*. Prides itself on serving the ultimate Wienerschnitzel, so big that it also offers half-portions for half-price, with wines from their own Heuriger vineyard. Daily 11am–10:30pm. (Closed August.)

Gösser Bierklinik $$ *1, Steindlgasse 4; Tel. 535 68 97*. This restaurant serves excellent food, located in a beautiful medieval building, which alone would make the visit worthwhile. Open Mon–Sat 10am–11:30pm.

Gräfin vom Naschmarkt $ *6, Linke Wienzeile 14; Tel. 586 33 89*. Right on the market place, serving Viennese staples all through the night, its heart-warming specialty, Goulash soup. Daily 6pm–8am.

Vienna

Griechenbeisl $$ *1, Fleischmarkt 11; Tel. 533 19 41.*
"Greek" only because that was its clientele a couple of hundred
years ago, today it serves traditional fare in one of Vienna's old-
est houses (1447), with lots of atmosphere. Enjoy the
Schanigarten. Daily 11am–1am.

Kervansaray-Hummerbar $$ *1, Mahlerstrasse 9; Tel.
512 88 43.* One of the best fish restaurants in town. Also
serves Turkish and international cuisine. Open Mon–Sat
noon–midnight.

Korso bei der Oper $$$ *1, Mahlerstrasse 2; Tel. 515 16 54
6. Haute cuisine,* accompanied by piano music, in the sumptu-
ous surroundings of the Hotel Bristol. Daily lunch, dinner
7pm–1am, closed Sat lunch.

Lucky Chinese $ *1, Kärntnerstrasse 24; Tel. 512 34 28.* If
you are looking for delicious Szechuan and Peking specialties,
then this is the place for you. Probably one of the best Chinese
restaurants in Vienna. Daily 11am–11pm.

Oswald und Kalb $$ *1, Bäckerstrasse 14; Tel. 512 1371.*
Fashionable upmarket Beisl, Styrian wine and cuisine, popular
with media people. Famous for its beef in vinegar and Styrian
pumpkin–seed oil. Daily dinner only 6pm–2am.

Palais Schwarzenberg $$$ *3, Hotel im Palais
Schwarzenberg; Schwarzenbergplatz 9; Tel. 798 45 15 600.*
Housed in a Baroque palace, this restaurant is truly unique with
a classic interior and a view over one of the most exquisite gar-
dens in town. Predominantly Austrian cuisine. Daily lunch
noon–2:30pm, dinner 6pm–11pm.

Palatschinkenkuchl $ *1, Köllnerhofgasse 4; Tel. 512 31 05*. Unpretentious, student atmosphere. Serves a variety of sweet and savory pancakes. Daily 10am–midnight.

Plachutta $$$ *1, Wollzeile 38; Tel. 512 15 77*. Exquisite service for definitive *haute cuisine* versions of Viennese specialities, especially a Tafelspitz fit for an emperor. Daily non-stop 11:30am–11:15pm.

Salzamt $$ *1, Ruprechtsplatz 1; Tel. 533 53 32*. A trendy bar/restaurant in Hermann Czech's stylish décor, frequented by writers, artists, and night-owls. Sophisticated treatment of old imperial delicacies. Daily dinner only 5pm–12:30am, bar till 4am.

Schnattl $$ *8, Lange Gasse 40; Tel. 405 34 0 0*. Good food and pleasant service in an area that is fast becoming a second center for Viennese restaurants. Excellent wine list. Open Mon–Fri 11:30am–2:30pm, 6pm–10pm; Sat/Sun dinner only 6pm–10pm.

Shalimar $ *6, Schmalzhofgasse 11; Tel. 596 43 17*. Vienna has only about a dozen Indian and Pakistani restaurants; this is one of the best. Daily noon–2:30pm, dinner 6pm–11pm.

Stadtbeisl $$ *1, Naglergasse 21; Tel. 533 35 07*. Old-fashioned interior with beautiful dark wood paneling. Large range of reasonably priced Viennese dishes. *Schanigarten*. Daily 10am–midnight.

Steirereck $$$ *3, Rasumofskygasse 2; Tel. 713 31 68*. Topnotch restaurant serving *Neue Wiener Küche* (Viennese nouvelle cuisine). Conservatory and pavement dining. *Wiener*

Vienna

Gabelfrühstück ("elevenses") served from 10:30am. Open Mon–Fri, lunch noon–2pm, dinner 7pm–midnight.

Trzesniewski $ *1, Dorotheergasse 1; Tel. 512 32 91*. Vienna's most famous sandwich bar, despite the uninviting exterior and unpronounceable name. No credit cards. 8:30am–7:30pm.

Vier Jahreszeiten $$$ *3, Johannesgasse 28; Tel. 711 22 14 3*. Inter-Continental Wien hotel's recently renovated Vier Jahreszeiten (Four Seasons) popular both with business executive and theater-goers. Open Mon–Fri lunch; dinner 7pm–midnight.

Weincomptoire $$ *1, Bäckerstrasse 6; Tel. 512 17 60*. As well as enjoying a selection of Viennese and other specialties, you can sample over 30 different wines by the glass, and a lot more by the bottle. Open Mon–Sat lunch; dinner 5pm–2am.

Zur Goldenen Glocke $$ *5, Kettenbrückengasse 8; Tel. 587 57 67*. Good, traditional Viennese cuisine at moderate prices, fresh produce from nearby Naschmarkt. Popular garden. Open Mon–Sat 11am–2:30pm, dinner 5:30pm–midnight.

Heuriger

10er Marie *16, Ottakringer Strasse 224; Tel. 409 4647*. A very old, very famous, and now very fashionable Heuriger. Popular hang-out amongst Viennese VIPs. Full menu. Year-round 3pm–midnight.

Bach-Hengl *19, Sandgasse 7, Grinzing; Tel. 320 24 39*. Family has been in business since 1137! Wine and meals in small and large rooms, children's playground. Year-round, 4pm–midnight.

Familie Muth *19, Probusgasse, Heiligenstadt; Tel. 370 22 47.* Boasts many prize-winning wines and its homemade fruit strudel pastry. Children's playground. Mid-Jan to mid-Dec 3:30pm–midnight, closed Tues.

Hans Sirbu *19, Kahlenberger Strasse 210; Tel. 320 59 28.* Picturesquely situated in the middle of Nussdorf vineyards. April to mid-Oct 3pm–midnight, closed Sun.

Weinhof Reichl *21, Stammersdorfer Strasse 41; Tel. 292 42 33.* Excellent family cuisine to go with its wines and Saturday music, in shady garden. Apr–Oct, Tue–Sun 2pm–midnight; Nov–Mar, Thu–Sun 2pm–midnight.

Weingur Reinprecht *19, Cobenzlgasse 22; Tel. 320 147 10.* Good Viennese music, fine wines and copious buffet meals in classical Grinzing setting make this a great experience. Mar–Nov, daily 3:30pm–midnight.

Stadtheuriger

Augustinerkeller *1, Augustinerstrasse 1; Tel. 533 10 26.* Huge, extremely lively *Stadtheuriger* in the heart of the First District. Suitable for large groups. Traditional music from 6:30pm. Daily 11am–midnight.

Melker Stiftskeller *1, Schottengasse 3.; Tel. 533 55 30.* Massive, cavernous vault belonging to Melk monastery, very good food and wine. Tues–Sat 5pm–midnight.

Urbanikeller *1, Am Hof 12.; Tel. 533 91 02.* Viennese cuisine in Baroque patrician house at patrician prices. Traditional Heuriger music every evening. Daily 6pm–1am.

Vienna

Zwölf-Apostel-Keller *1, Sonnenfelsgasse 3; Tel. 512 67 77.* Deep 17th-century cellars on three levels. Limited menu, but always crowded nonetheless. Try the black-currant wine — delicious and extremely potent!

Cafés

Alt Wien *1, Bäckerstrasse 9; Tel. 512 52 22.* Café bordering on *Beisl* with a deliberately decadent and dingy atmosphere. It offers an excellent and mouth-watering selection of snacks. Interesting literary clientele in the evenings.

Bräunerhof *1, Stallburggasse 2; Tel. 512 38 93.* This traditional and typical Viennese café serves very good food. Chamber music concerts are held here on weekends 3–6pm.

Central *1, Herrengasse 14, (Palais Ferstel); Tel. 533 37 63/26.* In renovated Palais Ferstel, smartly redecorated in an attempt to regain its former glory as a major literary café. Leon Trotsky was a regular visitor, and celebrated Austrian writer Peter Altenberg practically lived here. It serves good quality, if rather expensive, food.

Demel *1, Kohlmarkt 14; Tel. 535 1717.* By appointment, pastry chef to the Habsburgs, (its jam jars still bear the imperial seal) this monument among cafés serves the daintiest delicacies in town — the price is less sweet.

Do & Co *1, Stephansplatz 12; Tel. 535 39 69.* Situated on the 6th floor of the Haas-Haus, this café has a superb view of Stephansdom. Coffee and delicious cakes, restaurant on 7th floor (see page 135).

Frauenhuber *1, Himmelpfortgasse 6; Tel. 512 43 23.* One of Vienna's oldest cafés and one of the prettiest. Extensive menu.

Recommended Restaurants

Hawelka *1, Dorotheergasse 6; Tel. 512 82 30*. Younger crowd has taken over from the old clientèle of artists and writers. Walls are decorated with paintings by artists who couldn't afford to pay.

Kleines Café *1, Franziskanerplatz 3*. This very pretty café was designed by Hermann Czech and provides an excellent example of "quiet" interior design.

Korb *1, Tuchlauben 10; Tel. 533 72 15*. Impressive selection of cakes and a good restaurant menu.

Landtmann *1, Dr-Karl-Lueger-Ring 4; Tel. 532 06 21*. The most prestigious (and one of most expensive) of the Ringstrasse cafés, founded in 1873. This was one of Sigmund Freud's favorite haunts, and the setting of Arthur Schnitzler's story *Leutnant Gustl*. Large terrace.

Museum *1, Friedrichstrasse 6; Tel. 586 52 02*. Traditional Viennese café has lost its original design by Adolf Loos, but is quite tastefully renovated. Small selection of snacks only. Literary clientele. Covered *Schanigarten*.

Prückel *1, Stubenring 24; Tel. 512 61 15*. Fine old Viennese café. Good choice of newspapers. Piano music from 7–10pm on Monday, Wednesday, Friday, and Sunday. Serves a full menu.

Sperl *6, Gumpendorfer Strasse 11; Tel. 586 41 58*. Popular with Franz Lehár, this café originally built in 1880 was hardly altered until its renovation in 1983. Reasonably priced food. Billiards and card tables.

Volksgarten *1, Burgring 1; Tel. 533 05 18 0*. Open-air café with small but delicious selection of cakes and various other dishes.

INDEX